Empowerment of Women in North-East India

BY THE SAME AUTHOR

Women Governance in Tripura (2008)

ABOUT THE AUTHOR

Dr. Bhola Nath Ghosh is M.A. (Sociology) and Ph.D. in Social Sciences. He was also awarded a certificate from the University of East Anglia, Norwich, United Kingdom for participating in the course, entitled, "Course on Monitoring, Evaluation and Project Analysis". Currently an Assistant Professor in Sociology, Indian Statistical Institute, Kolkata. He presented several papers in national and international conferences which were held in India and abroad (United Kingdom, Bangladesh, Hungary and Sweden). Member of the Editorial Board of a Journal, namely, *South Eastern Anthropologist*, published from Ranchi and Jharkhand. He published several articles in national and international reputed journals. He authored and edited ten scholarly books and contributed several articles to various reputed Journals in the country and abroad. His areas of interest are Gender Issues, Panchayati Raj and Rural Development and social problem. He taught Sociology in Indian Statistical Institute for the last fifteen years and visiting faculty in West Bengal State University, Rabindra Bharati University and Jadavpur University.

Empowerment of Women in North-East India

By

Bhola Nath Ghosh
Sociological Research Unit
Indian Statistical Institute
Kolkata 700 108

CONCEPT PUBLISHING COMPANY PVT. LTD.,
NEW DELHI-110059

ISBN-13 : 978-93-5125-104-0

First Published 2015

Published and Printed by

Concept Since 1974

Concept Publishing Company Pvt. Ltd.
A/15-16, Commercial Block, Mohan Garden
New Delhi-110059 (India)
T: 25351460, 25351794, *F*: 091-11-25357109
E: publishing@conceptpub.com, W: www.conceptpub.com
Editorial Office: H-13, Bali Nagar, New Delhi-110 015, India.

Cataloging in Publication Data—*Courtesy:* D.K. Agencies (P) Ltd. <docinfo@dkagencies.com>

Ghosh, Bhola Nath, 1954-
Empowerment of women in North-East India / by Bhola Nath Ghosh.
p. cm.
Includes bibliographical references (p.) and index.
ISBN 9789351251040

1. Women in development—India—Tripura. 2. Women in development—India—Meghalaya. 3. Women—India—Tripura—Social conditions. 4. Women—India-Meghalaya—Social conditions. 5. Women—India—Tripura—Economic conditions. 6. Women—India—Meghalaya—Economic conditions. I. Title.

DDC 305.4209541 23

Foreword

India has pledged itself to gender equality through several articles of the Constitution. In fulfilment of this constitutional mandate, several steps have also been taken since independence to empower women. But nearly sixty years after women's rights were enshrined in the democratic fabric of India, we are yet to fully honour our constitutional commitments. Indian women in general, do not have equal rights as men in either political, social or economic spheres: they are discriminated against in education and in jobs; they are not equally represented in public institutions; they do not enjoy equal pay for equal work; and violence against women in both public and the private spheres is increasing. In this context the author's endeavour to capture the pace and perception as well as the process of empowerment of women in two North-Eastern States, Meghalaya and Tripura, deserves commendation. Selection of North-Eastern States, far away from mainland Kolkata, for conducting this study reflects author's keen interest to know and to make know the isolated and so called lesser States of our country.

The book is the outcome of tenacious academic exercise of the author which has encompassed the areas of social, cultural, economic, political, health, religious and environmental issues relating to empowerment of women in four remotest villages of Meghalaya and Tripura which reveals a lot of facts. The approach of the book is empirical with current database. The Author's style of introducing the States as background of understanding the study is brief but very catchy.

The author has touched upon various vital issues relating to economic empowerment of women. Issues like employment opportunities for women, displacement of female labour in agriculture, off-farm agricultural employment generation, problem of unemployment among the educated middle class, significance skill formation and training, etc., have received their due focus in the present research. Apart from this, the author has made an insightful observation of socio-cultural and also political issues like literacy and education among women, participation of women in decision making.

In relation to this, the author has presented an extremely interesting enquiry into the traditionally matrilineal Meghalayan society as to why women still remain out of decision making institutions at all levels. Comparative analysis between the women in Meghalaya and Tripura on these aspects has made the book further attractive.

The situational analysis of empowerment of women in two North-Eastern States duly supported with several tables and charts provides an in-depth analysis of the status of empowerment. The suppression of women from participation in social, political and economic life hurts the people as a whole, not just women. Women's empowerment, therefore, is crucial to the overall development of the society in large. The author's work, significantly, acts as a foundation for further planning and implementation of related projects in Meghalaya and Tripura.

This book is an important addition to the literature on women studies in this region and has great value to the academic community, social activists, women agencies, policy makers and administrators. I sincerely hope that Dr. Bholanath Ghosh's efforts will be appreciated and valued for its substance and practical significance.

Agartala
10th October, 2008

Dr. Tapati Chakravarti
Chairperson,
Tripura Commission for Women

Foreword

The book on "Empowerment of Women in North East with special reference to the two States Tripura and Meghalaya" is one of the pioneering study of the Indian Statistical Institute Calcutta conducted by Dr. Bholanath Ghosh. It deserves special compliment. The comparative field study of the two States relating to the empowerment of women has touched upon the different aspects of the social, cultural and economic life of the women. The material has highlighted the social set-up of both the patrilineal and matrilineal society.

The book will be a resourceful material for those interested in women studies.

Prof. Biloris Lyndem
Chairperson
Meghalaya State
Commission for Women

Acknowledgements

I am thankful to the honourable members of Technical Advisory Committee (TAC) and Divisional Committee of Scientific Workers (DCSW) of the Social Sciences Division of Indian Statistical Institute, Kolkata for kindly allowing me to undertake the study.

Though the idea to take up the issue of women empowerment primarily emanated from my subjective experience as a student of Sociology having a first hand knowledge in this field of work, I would like to put on record my sincere gratitude to them who encourage me to nurture it and also help me in various ways to complete me the writing. My debts of gratitude are many.

Various individuals and officials of different Government departments and other organizations in Tripura and Meghalaya were kind enough to extend their co-operation to this humble endeavour. I am grateful to all of them. I also received full co-operation from Library of North-Eastern Council, Library of I.C.S.S.R., Library of North-Eastern Hill University, Shillong and Library of Tripura University, State Library of Tripura, Library of I.S.I. for the collection of data and other information. For all of them I express my deep gratitude.

I thank to Prof. Manoranjan Pal and Prof. P. Bharati, Indian Statistical Institute, Kolkata and Dr. Utpal Kumar De, North-Eastern Hill University who inspire me to conduct the study and help me in different stages of the work.

I would like to thank Ms. Rebeka Khatoon, Mr. Md. Salim resident of Agartala (Tripura State) and Mr. Krow resident of Shillong (Meghalaya State) for helping me in the collection of field data.

I thank to Dr. Debashis Bhattacharya who went once with me in the field of Shillong for conducting the field survey. I thank to Dr. Susmita Bharati and Ms. Suparna Shome to help me in time to time when required.

I thank to Sri Rabindra Nath Jana, Sonali Chakraborti and Dr. Tirthankar Ghosh, Mr. Kamalakhya Das of ISI, Kolkata for their help in different ways.

I express my gratitude to Prof. B. Dutta Ray, Secretary, NEICSSR, Shillong; Prof. Sirajul Ahmed, Bengali Department and Prof. Mahadev Chakraborty, Dept. of History, Tripura University, Tripura; and Prof. Nikhlesh Kumar and Dr. A.K Nongkynrih, Department of Sociology, North-Eastern Hill University, Shillong, Meghalaya, who spared their valuable time and gave important suggestions and comments.

I take this privilege to put it on record my deep sense of indebtedness to Prof. Tapati Chakravarti, Chairperson, Tripura State Commission for Women, Tripura and Prof. Biloris Lyndem, Chairperson, Meghalaya State Commission for Women, Meghalaya, for writing a foreword to this book in spite of their pressing engagements. I am also grateful to them for their creative suggestions and comments.

I thank Mr. Chayan Roy Choudhury and Mr. Rajib Choudhury to help in different times for handling and analyzing the data.

I thank the B.D.O. (Sri Aninda Bhattacharya) and Bhaskar Bhattacharjee, Secretary of Jirania block; Haridas Sarkar and Adhir Mohan Dutta, Pradhan and Upopradhan of Paschim Noabadi Gram Panchayat respectively; and Sri Debasis Modok, Additional Subdivisional Magistrate, Bishalgar district of West Tripura, Tripura; Srimati Punima Sangma, B.D.O of Mawlyngknanng; Sri Shanaih Khonsgsti, Gram Sevak (Ringkseh and Kyton-u-Mon villages); and Sri Medistae Warbah (Chairman of Nongkrem Darbar, Khyrim Syiem Ship, who is inhabitant of Kyton-u-Mon village) who provided all informations, hospitality, security, and mental support. Without their cooperation, it was not possible to collect the information from the fields, as we know all of our studied villages of both of the States having the insurgency.

I am greatly indebted to the villagers of Beltali and Kalitila of Tripura and Ringkseh and Kyton-u-Mon of Meghalaya for their attention and kind co-operation, which enabled me to conduct this study and without whose co-operation, I would not have written a line. However, I would like to take the whole responsibility for any error remaining in my study.

Before I would conclude, I would like to record my sincere thanks to my colleagues in the Sociological Research Unit of Indian Statistical Institute for their help.

Kotkata
21st May, 2008

Bhola Nath Ghosh

Preface

Women's empowerment as a phenomenon is not something new. Discipline of social science is moving into new horizons with empowerment and development of women becoming important aspect of social science. Social, Economic and Political development can be achieved fully when the society recognizes women as one among social partners, provides equal rights, facilitates them with equal education, health and allow them to participate equally and effectively in all social functions and delivered in the decision making process. Therefore, studies on the subject related to the issues on women are gaining importance from all corners day-by-day. The main force behind women studies is the movement to assert the interest of women in the society. It does not mean the domination of women over their counterpart men; rather it is a need to restore the half of human beings in the rightful place in society.

The simple dictionary, the meaning of the word 'empowerment' is giving somebody power or authority to act. Yet it has got its own significance. It has beyond the simple meaning that prompted the present studies.

Empowerment of women is essentially a broader concept heralding a shift from unjust to just, subservient to successful, passive to active ability and entity for women. In the broader context, empowerment of women refers to questioning social, economic and political discrepancies and distortions in terms of gender. By process of empowerment, we mean activities through which the women get access to power so that their wishes are materialised. It is the complex interplay of various factors like social, economic, political, psychological, physical and attitudinal and so on. However, "empowerment" has different meaning to different actors in the development fields. The issues of women's empowerment is closely associated with women's development, but unfortunately, there was no such constructive thinking about women's empowerment in India till Fifth Five Year Plan (1974-79) at Government level. Of course, the National Committee on the status of women was set up in 1971 before the declaration of women decade. This committee submitted their report towards equality in 1974. Also, almost each state has one women's commission to look after the problems and grievances of the women.

The year 2001 was declared as the "International Women's Empowerment Year" by the United Nations. Simultaneously, Govt. of India has also recognized the same year as the "Women's Empowerment Year".

Therefore, this book takes into consideration of the issues of empowerment of women in theoretically and empirically. It may therefore, be a good acquisition of various institutional libraries as well as individuals researchers and social workers who have been engaged in the studies and research related to the gender issues. It would also be a great help to the student, researcher, teacher in the academic and research institutions.

Bhola Nath Ghosh

Contents

List of Tables

List of Figures

1
Introduction

Empowerment is a multifaceted, multi-dimensional and multilayered concept. It is the action and interaction of various factors—physical, socioeconomic, political, psychological, attitudinal and so on. Empowerment means the access of a person to that kind of power that would enable him or her to fulfil his/her wishes. In the development field, the word 'empowerment' has different meanings for different actors. However, since women are the principal gender group that this research study concerns itself with, we shall mainly touch upon the issue of empowerment in relation to women. The year 2001 was declared as the "International Women's Empowerment Year" by the United Nations. Simultaneously the Government of India also recognised the same year as the 'Year of Women's Empowerment'.

Without a doubt, the issue of women's empowerment is closely associated with the development of women, but unfortunately, there was no such constructive thinking about women's empowerment in India at the government level till the Fifth Five Year Plan (1974-79). Of course, the National Committee on the Status of Women was set up in 1971, before the declaration of the Women's Decade. This committee submitted its report "Towards Equality" in 1974. In recent years, the empowerment of women is a popular and much discussed issue, but the very term 'empowerment' is the buzzword since the 1960s.

Since 1990, the empowerment of women has become a slogan, a craze and there is reference to it in almost every literature and matter concerned with women's issues, not to mention the women's development programmes.

The original concept of empowerment as espoused by Paulo Freire did not include the gender gamut. It is only after the feminists picked up the concept that it gained wide currency. Paulo Freire expounded the notion of "conscientization" as the process by which the poor could challenge the existing structure of power and then gradually gain power and control from the powerful; in other words, the poorer and deprived sections of a given society could thus take control of their lives. Thus empowerment is believed to be an enabling process for the full and active participation of the oppressed people in the formulation, execution and evolution of decisions determining the functions and efficiencies for the society.

The empowerment of women is essentially a broader concept heralding a shift from the unjust to the just, the subservient to the successful, and from the passive to the active ability and entity for women. In the broader context, the empowerment of women refers to the questioning of the social, economic and political discrepancies and distortions, in terms of gender. As an enabling concept for women, it pertains to challenging her own subjugation and thereafter gaining control over the resources of every conceivable sphere, in the process transforming radically the structural, systematic and institutional inequalities through her own participation, priorities and perspectives. Thus it is a process where women can gain access, have space and scope to examine and extricate their lives and gender relations critically and collectively. This is a collective effort and individual endeavour is not often likely to meet with success. Moreover, the term "women's empowerment" has come to be associated with all women's struggle for social justice and equality.

The process of empowerment deals with how to increase capacity of women and what they need to become empowered. First they must be provided with and should get fulfilled certain essential needs. These basic needs could be provided through welfare services. Equal access to resources like educational opportunities, credit and property is the next step in the process of empowerment. Creating awareness among women about the existing gender discrimination, gender inequality is most important in empowering them. Then, they must recognize that their problems stem from Inherent structural and institutional discrimination.

The empowerment process in the developed country is different from that of developing nations of Third World. It is more strategical, i.e., changing patriarchal norms, gender division of labour, gaining equality and changing attitudes of society towards women in the developed countries. While in the developing nations, it is more focused on to meet the basic needs, increase in income, educating and give training in skill development to meet along with strategic gender needs. Meeting both practical needs and strategic interests are necessary to empower women. Women are the main caretakers in the families below the poverty line. Women contribute to the household income. Hence, practical needs of these women related to daily life—food, housing, income, health care and welfare benefits ought to be met. But mere meeting practical needs do not empower women unless strategic interests are fulfilled. Strategic interests are long term and almost common to all women. They are related to improving women's position that include action to increase women's knowledge and skills, give them legal protection, provide equal opportunities/participation on decision making and greater access to resources, etc. Strategic interests transform gender relations and empower women.

Empowerment also means having choices and women's ability to make choices. Women must be made to recognize the choices they have, enable them to make choices. For example, education is one of the choices, women must be made aware of the importance of education and choices in the form of education available; opportunity must be given and they will make the best use of choices.

Equal participation of women in the decision-making leads to their empowerment. It could be achieved through mobilization and organization of women through all levels. Increasing consciousness and awareness building is the important component of the process of empowerment. First women must recognize the ideology that legitimizes domination and then understand how it perpetuates their oppression. Then try to change values and attitudes, which are "anti-women" that most women have internalized since their childhood. So self-consciousness and awareness must arise in each individual women to empower themselves. But this self-consciousness and awareness does not come spontaneously, so is empowerment. Changing other women's consciousness must externally induce it. Altering self-image and

beliefs about rights and capabilities could create consciousness among other women. Awareness of gender discrimination challenging the sense of inferiority, recognizing the value of their labour and their contribution to the society and conscientisation will empower women.

2

Objectives and Aims of the Study

The basic objective of the study is to understand the pace and perception as well as the process of empowerment of the women belonging to different categories of the rural societies in Meghalaya and Tripura. As such, the specific aims of the study are:

(a) To identify the aspiration and analyze the performance of different sections of women in the villages;
(b) To examine the process of empowerment of women in terms of social, cultural, economic, political, religious, legal, health and environmental aspects; and
(c) To identify the limitations and successes of the women who had set their goals in terms of empowerment.

3
Area of the Study

The researcher has identified two specific areas located in the north-eastern part of India as the area of the study. Precisely, Meghalaya and Tripura are the two north-eastern States where the study has been conducted. Two villages have been purposively selected from each of the States. In Tripura, the two villages that have been identified as the area of the study are Beltali and Kalitila, both being located under the Paschim Noabadi Gram Panchayat of Jirania block, West Tripura district. The two villages in Meghalaya wherein the research study has been conducted are Ringkseh and Kyton-u-Mon under the East Khasi Hill district of Mawlyngknang block. The Khasi Hill district of Meghalaya, which consists of 858 inhabited villages under 8 blocks, has a population of 6,60,923.

All the above locations are primarily inhabited by different categories of rural societies.

Interestingly, we have focused on these two States in particular because of the contrasting situations therein, for while in one State (Meghalaya), the 73rd Amendment has not yet been implemented, in the other State (Tripura), the above Amendment has been implemented.

A Few Words about Tripura

Tripura, an erstwhile princely state, acceded to the Indian Union on 15th October 1949. Following the accession, the State came to be administered as a Union Territory. Later, after the passing of the North-East Areas (reorganization) Act on 30th December 1971, Tripura attained full-fledged statehood on 21st January 1972.

The State of Tripura is bordered by Bangladesh on the west, south and north, Assam on the north-east and Mizoram on the east. The State is connected with the rest of India by only one road, which runs through the hills to the borders of Cachar district in Assam.

The State is situated in the extreme south-west of the north-eastern region and spreads over an area of 10,492 sq. km. About 70 per cent of the total areas of the State is hilly, leaving very little area cultivable. About 60 per cent of the total area of the State is classified as 'forest' under the ambit of the Forest Conservation Act. Despite being geographically the smallest State of the north-eastern region, it is the second most populous State in the region after Assam. The present population is estimated to be about 32 lakh.

The demographic composition of the State underwent significant changes with its long record of historical transformations. As such, till independence it was a tribal majority State (approximately 56% in 1921 and about 51% in 1931 and 1941). Subsequently, owing to the influx of people from across the border, the tribals in the State were reduced to a minority. According to the Census of India 2001, the population composition of the State is thus: 31 per cent tribal, 16 per cent SC, about 30 per cent OBC and the rest are others (Provisional Population Totals).

Although the original tribal population have their own language, today about 80 per cent of the State's inhabitants, including the tribals, use Bengali in their day-to-day conversation while going about with their duties. Almost all Tripuris can speak and understand Bengali. Besides Bengali, the other languages that are used here are Tripuri, Chakma, Burma, etc.

Old or *puran* Agartala was the capital of Tripura since the time of Maharaja Krishna Manikya (1760-83) who had shifted the capital from Udaipur to this place.

The Ujjayann Palace is situated in the heart of Agartala town. The Palace has recently been acquired by the State government and it presently houses the Legislative Assembly, besides a few Government offices.

Agartala became the capital of the State during the time of Maharaja Krishnakishore Manikya (1830-50) and since then it has remained the seat of the State headquarters. Maharaja Birendra Kishore Manikya (1909-23), who was also a good artist, is said to have himself prepared the plan of the Palace and built the Kunjaban Palace of Agartala.

For the sake of information only it may be mentioned that the great poet of Bengal, Rabindranath Tagore, stayed in the eastern apartment of this famous Palace during his seventh and last visit to Agartala in 1926. One could get a distinct view of the Baramura Hills in the eastern horizon from the encompassing (*gol*) verandah attached to this eastern part. This verandah has been the "mute witness to many a dear moments" when the poet composed a few popular songs (all incorporated in the Vaikali series).

A Few Words about Meghalaya

The word *'Meghalaya'* is derived from the words *'Megh'* and *'alay'* which combine to denote 'the abode of the clouds'. The name is most appropriate for the State as the skies above the hills remain covered with clouds of different hues of white and grey throughout the year from season to season. Fogs, mists and nimbus clouds loom large during the rainy season and at other times too patches of cumulus and stratus clouds are seen floating overhead the high hills. The State was given this name by the renowned scholar Dr. Suniti Kumar Chatterjee, Professor Emiritus, Calcutta University.

Meghalaya, is one of the States that are combinedly known as the "Seven Sisters of the north-east of India" and it covers an area of 300 kilometres (approximately) in length and about 100 kilometres (approximately) in breadth. It is surrounded by Assam on the north and the east and by Bangladesh on the south and the west. The districts of Goalpara, Kamrup, Nagaon and Karbi Anglong in Assam share their borders with Meghalaya in the north while the Cachar and North Cachar districts of Assam have a common border with the State in the east.

The capital of Meghalaya, Shillong lies on the eastern part of the State. The city stretches for about 6 km on an elevated tract. Tracing back its history, we come to learn that it was a small village until 1864, when it became the new civil station of the Khasi and Jaintia Hills. In 1874, following the formation of the commissioner's province, it was chosen as the capital of the new administration.

The principal languages in Meghalaya are Khasi and Garo with English as the official State language.

The magical valley of Meghalaya lies between 20°1′ N to 20°5′ N latitude and 85°49′ E to 92°52′ E longitude.

4

Justification of the Study

It is felt that keeping in mind the situational differences in the two States where the study has been conducted, it is worth to see the variation in the process of empowerment of women in Tripura (where the society is basically patrilineal and 33 per cent of the seats in Gram Panchayat have been reserved for the women) and Meghalaya (where the society is primarily matrilineal but due to very little scopes for the political affiliation of women, seats have not yet been reserved for them in the Gram Panchayat).

It may be recalled here that prior to independence the situation of women in rural India was one that allowed them virtually no freedom. It is only after the 73rd Amendment to the Constitution of India that the Indian women have been allotted one-third of the total number of seats in the local self-government bodies in the rural areas. It is, therefore, worthwhile to assess the extent to which this Amendment could alter the lives of the rural Indian women, at least in the region where the ruling on women's representation in self-government is being implemented.

Different categories of women may perceive empowerment differently due to their own social positions. By categories we mean, socio-political and economic strata to which they belong. Women's empowerment may, therefore, mean differently during the different stages of development.

It is felt that this study would add to the existing body of knowledge about the social, political and economic situation of women in the different communities, in terms of their entitlement and their present status. It would also have policy implications that might help the government and Non-Governmental Organizations in drawing community action plans in their attempt to ensure women's welfare.

5

Literature Review

According to the Country Report of the Government of India[1] (1995) presented in the fourth World Congress on Women, Beijing, 1995, "empowerment means moving from a position of enforced powerlessness to own power; it would promote women's inherent strength and positive self-image." Nath and Chatterjee[2] (1966) stated that empowerment is most significant in the control of ideology, i.e., control over thoughts and perceptions that shape individual beliefs, values and attitudes. Sharma[3] (1991-92) pointed out that "the term empowerment refers to a range of activities from individual self-assertion to collective resistance, protest and mobilization that challenge basic power relations".

The Chairperson of the National Commission for Women once observed: "One does not get empowerment just by being given powers and receiving them. Until we have an inner realization, until we believe in our strength and exert it, we cannot be truly empowered." Parthasarathi[4] (2002).

Discrimination across gender is the most distressing fact of such deprivation cutting across caste, class and ethnic composition [De Haan[5] (1994)]. The gender discrimination is omnipresent in all societies, whether feudal or capitalist.

In many societies, especially in the rural areas, it is the women who take the responsibility of fetching drinking water and collecting fuel wood even as they participate in gardening and agricultural activities, ranging from sowing to harvesting. Their role either as a mother or as a wife, in addition to the other Socio-economic performances, has immense importance in the welfare and wellbeing of the society. In the process of ensuring the wellbeing of the family, women as known to make many sacrifices as well. As for instance, sometimes in the very poor (low income) families, when there is not enough food, the women try hard to fulfil the nutritional needs of the male members, the children and the elderly, while they themselves sustain without the required nutritional intake. Unfortunately, such kinds of sacrifices by the women go unnoticed by the male members, as a result of which they are not given their due recognition. Consequent to this, in most cases, because of the lack of recognition and, may be, due to the nature of their work and non-marketing of their contribution, the proper evaluation of the different activities by the women have never been done. Their contribution to the society is no less than their male counterparts. Some researchers and famous sociologists have even opined that the women's role in the traditional societies was more comprehensive, active, independent and valued (Hamilton[6], 1981; Schreiner[7], 1978).

Despite the importance of their contribution to the society, in the earlier days, women were strictly not allowed to take part in any decision-making. Even as of today, in the traditional societies like that of many tribal societies in North-East India, where the females exert significant control over most of the economic activities, they are not allowed to take part in the *Dorbars* or village council meeting. There too, the headman of a cluster of population is invariably a male person and all major decisions are taken by him and the other influential men in the council.

Historical evidences show that in the very early stages of our society, women were regarded with reverence as Mother Goddess (*Shakti*)—a symbol of life with the immense capacity of tolerance and sacrifice. Hence, the then women had a respectful place in the society (Menon,[8] 1975). In the ancient *Rig Vedic* period too, women used to be regarded as the co-partners in life, in all pleasures and hazards, enjoying the joys and tolerating the sorrows together (Thomas, 1964)[9].

However, with time, the position of women in India underwent a sea change, which degraded their position to that below the menfolk. If we take a glimpse into the Indian history, we find rich evidences of the subjugation of women during and since Mughal rule. Perhaps the concept of *purdah* for women and that of child marriage left a deep impact on the socio-cultural life of India, irrespective of religion, caste and creed, weakening extensively the social position of women in particular.

Much later in pre-independence India, social reformers like Raja Ram Mohan Roy and Ishwar Chandra Vidyasagar made the efforts to bring about concrete changes in women's social position. While some successful efforts were made by Raja Ram Mohan Roy to abolish the inhuman custom of Sati, Ishwar Chandra Vidya Sagar directed his efforts for the remarriage of widows. Despite widespread protests and differences in opinion among different sections of the societies, laws were passed to treat the act of *Sati* a crime, as well as to make provisions for the remarriage of widows. The social reformers fought tooth and nail to raise the age of marriage, especially for girls, in order to remove the evils of child marriage and set the base for female education. (The Child Marriage Restraint Act was passed in 1929 where the minimum age of marriage for girls was fixed at 14 years. Later the age was again raised to 18 years in the Special Marriage Act 1954) (Kapadia, 1966)[10].

Although the provision for the education of women was legalized long back, due to the rigidity of our social structure and the predominance of the males and guided by the conservative religious strictures, the women were for long not allowed to step into the realm of education. It is only after the government's efforts towards attaining the status of 'Literate India' that the departments of education, at the State and central levels, started giving impetus to female education.

Ghosh and De[11] (2002) have shown that if the women members or Panchayat Pradhan are educated and have the independent decision-making capability, then the performance of the Panchayat is bound to improve. By now it is an accepted fact that the women in general are less corrupted. Chattopadhyay and Duflo[12] (2001) have also explained the impact of having women in Panchayat administration, either as members or as the Pradhan. From the results of their primary survey, they found that the Panchayats having women Pradhans give more emphasis on infrastructure development, adult education and building education infrastructure. Also, in the Panchayat meetings, they stress more on women's issues, like health care for mother and children, problem of nutrition, and so on.

An interesting observation made by Devendra[13] (1993) is that a woman receives respect and care in her family only after she gives birth to a male child. To a large extent then, a woman's status in the family is governed by the number of sons she gives birth to.

Just a few decades earlier, politics and matters relating to it, were largely dominated by the menfolk, with only a few privileged women—mostly of the stature of Indira Gandhi, Vijayalakshmi Pandit, Sarojini Naidu, to name a few, joining the political camp and coming to the forefront. However, it was felt gradually that women from the grassroots level had an equally important role to play in the political process for ensuring growth and development. So, with a view to motivate women's participation in the political affairs of their immediate localities so that they could simultaneously get engaged in the developmental activities in their areas, the government legalized the reservation of seats for women in the Panchayat, municipal bodies, State Assembly and Parliament as well. In this context however Madhu Kishwar[14] (1996) argues that the present scheme of reservation will *ghettoise* women's politics, confining them to contesting only from the reserved constituencies. She further maintains that the lottery system of gender-based reservation would inhibit the women from nursing their constituency, which could damage the legitimacy of women's participation.

The World Bank believes that with the advancing gender equality, governments could greatly enhance the future well-being and prosperity of their people[15]. In fact the Bank is correct when it states that no efforts at gender equality can be successful without the participation of the women themselves.[16]

Singh and Pundir[17] observed that the main reasons behind women's political marginalisation are—"tradition, physiology, lack of vertical mobility, concern for home and family, psychology and lack of patronage, particularly from senior women politicians.

The Committee on the status of women in India, in its report (1974) *Towards Equality*[18] observed that though women do not numerically constitute a minority, they are beginning to acquire the features of a minority community by the recognized dimensions: inequality of class (economic situation) status (social position) and political power.

Ghosh[19] focused on the role of women as decision makers and called for eliminating gender bias by ensuring equal opportunities for them through focus points: parity, power, participation and partnership.

Kishwar[20] argues that the present scheme of reservation will *ghettoise* women's politics—confining them to contesting only from the reserved constituencies. He further maintains that the lottery system of gender-based reservation would inhibit women from nursing their constituency, which would damage the legitimacy of women's participation.

According to *Srivastava*[21], given the frantic preference for a male child in India every year about four million women risk their lives and get illegal abortion done. Many pregnant women die in the process but their deaths are never reported by their family members or by those who carry out these sex selective abortions.

According to *Altekar*[22] *(1962)*, Women used to enjoy considerable freedom in their personal life and had the access to education and thus the society had due respect to them. They were also familiar with social and political life and playing a significant role in those matters.

Women would attend meeting along with men, as stated by *Sharma*[23] *(1968)*.

In cultured families well-behaved and talented daughters were regarded as the pride of those families as stated by *Kumarasambhava*[24].

Women were not actively involved in political activities and were not part of the *sabha* as was in *Rig Vedic* period as argued by *Jayal*[25] *(1996); Atharva veda*[26]

Due to the interference of Mughals and Britishers, many matriarchal societies have been disintegrated as observed by *Jeffry*[27] *(1993); Jharta*[28] *(1998)*.

According to De and Ghosh[29] (2002), there are ample empirical evidences that supports the idea that improvement of several indicators like literacy rate, education (general and professional), access to opportunities, occupational structure, working conditions, participation in cultural and decision making processes as well as holding of assets raise the social status of women and finally the well-being through the reduction in fertility rate, maternal mortality and promoting rapid implementation of family planning programme and thus controlling population growth.

Many women in third world countries have had birth control forced on them where sterilizations were administered without their knowledge and concerns for risk to health as argued by Bulbeck[30] (1998).

The first phase of western struggle is on the understanding that the key to the better life is a better education, lower birthrate and equality of women as stated by Picard[31] (1986).

According to Bulbeck[32] (1988), the western women's political strategies of education of women, lower birth rates for the security of better health and equality of gender are also assumed to be appropriate for women of the third world nations.

But one thing is common to all feminist movements against the patriarchal structures is that in every society women are subordinate to men at least in some respects as said by Bulbeck[33] (1988).

During the post Second World War the major concern of the movement was the sexual liberalization and the right to paid work and equal rewards for it as an escape from household drudgery as stated by Bulbeck[34] (1988).

According to Norris and Inglehart[35] (2000), compared to economic opportunities, education and legal rights, political participation is the area in which the gender gap has narrowed during 1995-2000.

The study by Vianello *et al.*[36] (1990) showed that a husband's power within marriage tended to increase in proportion to the resources that he could muster: education, income, prestige, social status and so on.

Burr[37] (1973) developed a general model of marital power, which spells out a set of proposition. It takes into account the complex interconnection between the amount of power, the cultural or normative context, and the specific tangible and intangible resources that affect the distribution of marital power.

Peattie and Rein[38] (1983) and Sapiro[39] (1984) rightly mentioned that it is necessary for women to organize themselves as women, and to devise a strategy on how to win leading positions.

Kabeer[40] (1999) has attempted to construct the indicators of the empowerment of women, by using three-dimensional conceptual framework: (a) the 'resources' as part of the pre-conditions of empowerment; (b) the agency as an aspect of process; and lastly (c) the achievements as a measure of outcomes. The study shows that the most probable indicators for empowerment of women are family structure, material advantage, financial autonomy, and freedom of movement and lifetime experience of employment participation in the modern sector.

The study by Malhotra and *et al.*[41] (2002) identifies the methodological approaches in measuring and analyzing the empowerment of women. The various indicators for measuring empowerment of women given in the study are: domestic decision-making; finance and resource allocation; social and domestic matters; child related issues; access to or control over resources; freedom of movement and so on.

Stine and Karina[42] (2003) explain the term 'empowerment' as a process by which the disempowered individuals and groups gain the power to control their lives and the ability to make strategic life choices.

Women, moreover, may not be visible in Parliament, not taking part in debates and raising issues pertinent to women: taking a stand only on those issues which do not conflict with the party's stand. An analysis of the parliament committees too reveals the low visibility of women in parliament. Except for the committee on the empowerment on women, which has mostly women members, almost all the rest have between zero to one women member and almost no committee has a women in the chair. (Najma Heptulla was the ex-officio Chairperson of a few committees in the Rajya Sabha and as well as the Chairperson of the committee on the Empowerment of Women).

The Draft National Policy for Empowerment of Women 1996 describes empowerment as follows:

> "A synergy of development measures will be affected and affirmative action designed for the holistic empowerment of women. Women will be given complete and equal access to and control over factors contributing to such empowerment, particularly, health, education, information, life long learning for self-development, vocational skills, employment and income earning opportunities, technical services, land and other forms of property, including through inheritance and matrimony, common property resources, credit, technology and markets, etc."

NOTES

1. Government of India (1995), Fourth World Congress on Women, Beijing, 1995, Country Report, Department of Women and Child Development, Ministry of Human Resource Development, p. 116.
2. Nath, Kamla, and Milly Chatterjee, (1996) Why Women? What Politics? Centre for Social Research, New Delhi, p. 4.
3. Sharma, Kumud, (1991-92) "Grass Root Organisations and Women's Empowerment: Some Issues in the Contemporary Debate", in Samya Shakti, Centre for Women's, p. 29. Development Studies, New Delhi, Vol. VI, p. 29.
4. Parthasarathi V. (2002), Inaugural Address on Women and Political Empowerment. Institute of Social Sciences. New Delhi. p. 17.
5. De Haan, Arjun, (1994), Bibliographical Review on Social Exclusion in South Asia, Amsterdam School for Social Research, Amsterdam, Netherlands, ILO.
6. Hamilton, Cicely (1981), *Marriage as a Trade,* Women's Press London.
7. Schreiner, Olive (1978) *Women and Labour,* Virago, London, p. 1.
8. Menon, L.D. (1975), "India and International Women's Year", *India Quarterly,* Vol. 31. No. 3, July-September, p. 278.
9. Thomas. P. (1964), *Indian Women through the Age,* Asia Publishing House, Bombay, p. 49.
10. Kapadia, K.M. (1966), *Marriage and Family in India,* Oxford University Press, Calcutta, pp. 154-156.
11. Ghosh, B. and U.K. De (2002), "Leadership and the Performance of Panchayats in Rural Development: An Experience from Tripura". Paper presented at the UGC National Seminar on 'Transformation in Rural Society', held at Tufanganj Mahavidyalaya, West Bengal, on 24-25 September, 2002.
12. Chattopadhyay, R. and E. Duflo (2001) "Women as Policy Maker: Evidence from a India-Wide Randomized Policy Experiment" downloaded from www.ssc.wisc.edu/~mbrown/chattopadhyay duflo_rev.pdf.
13. Devendra, Kiran, "Sex Discrimination: Before and Birth", in Girl Child and Family Violence, ed. Pramila Kapur, New Delhi: Har Anand Publications.
14. Madhu Kishwar in Munshi, http://www.freespeech.org/manushi/96/ zenana.html.
15. Choksi, Armeane M., *Forward in Toward Gender Equality,* World Bank Publications, Washington D.C., U.S.A., (1995), p.viii.
16. The World Bank, *Toward Gender Equality, The Role of Public Policy,* A World Bank Publications, Washington D.C., 1995, p. 2.
17. Singh, Pitam and J.K. Pundir; "Women Legislators in U.P. Background, Emergence and Role", *Economic and Political Weekly,* Vol. XXXVII, No. 10, March 9 to 15, 2002, p. 923.

18. The Committee on the Status of Women's *"Towards Equality"*, published in 1974, p. 301.
19. Ghosh, Archana; *"Women's Reservation in Urban Local Bodies, Perspective from Chennai Municipal Corporation Election 2001"*, Urban Management, The Institute of Local Government and Urban Studies (ILGUS), Kolkata, October, 2002, p. 42.
20. Kishwar, Madhu in *Manushi*, http://www.freespeech.org/manushi/96/zenna.html
21. Srivastava, Radhika D.D; Desire for a boy drives them to quacks for a quick abortion, *The Times of India*, Friday, July 28, 2000, New Delhi-13.
22. Altekar, A.S. (1962); *The Position of Women in Hindu Civilization*, Motilal Banarasidass, Delhi, p. 339.
23. Sharma, R.S. (1968); Aspects *of Political Ideas and Institutions in Ancient India*, Motilal Banarasidass, Delhi, p. 54-61.
24. Kumarasambhava, VI, 63. Also quoted Altekar, *op cit.*, p. 4.
25. Jayal, S. (1996); *The Status of Women in the Epics*, Motilal Banarasidass, Delhi.
26. *Atharva Veda* VIII 10.5, quoted in R.S. Sharma (1968), *Aspects of Political Ideas and Institutions in Ancient India*, Motilal Banarasidass, Delhi, p. 103.
27. Jeffry, Robin (1993); *Policies Women and Wellbeing: How Kerala became a Model*, Oxford University Press Ch-2, pp. 34-71.
28. Jharta, Bhawana (1998); *Women and Politics in India*; Deep & Deep Publications, New Delhi, p. 53.
29. Ghosh, B. and De, U.K. (2002); *"Leadership and the Performance of Panchayats in Rural Development: An Experience from Tripura"*, paper presented at the UGC National Seminar on Transformation in Rural Society, held at Tufangunj Mahavidyalaya, West Bengal, on 24-25 September, 2002.
30. Chilla, Bulbeck (1988); *One World's Women's Movement*, Pluto Press, London, p. 1, Census of India, Various Issues.
31. Picard, Andre (1986); "of JR and Condoms" *New Intertionalist*, No. 156, February, p. 3.
32. Chilla, Bulbeck (1988); *One World's Women's Movement*, Pluto Press, London, p. 2, Census of India, Various Issues.
33. Chilla, Bulbeck (1988); *One World's Women's Movement*, Pluto Press, London, p. 3, Census of India, Various Issues.
34. Chilla, Bulbeck (1988); One World's Women's Movement, Pluto Press, London, p. 5, Census of India, Various Issues.
35. Norris, P. and Inglehart, R. (2000); *"Cultural Barriers to Women's Leadership: A Worldwide Comparison"*, IPSA, 2000, Paper.
36. Vianello, Mino and Siemienska, Renata (1990); *Gender Inequality: A Comparative Study of Discrimination and Participation*, New Delhi, SAGE Publications.

37. Burr, W.R. (1973); *Theory Construction and The Sociology of the Family,* Wiely Publications.
38. Peattie, L. and Rein, M. (1983); *Women's Claims: A Study in Political Economy*: Oxford University Press: London.
39. Sapiro. V. (1984); *The Political Integration of Women*: University of Illinonis Press.
40. Kabeer, N. (1999); "The Conditions and Consequences of Choice: Reflection on the Measurement of Women's Empowerment", UNRISD Discussion Paper No. 108, August.
41. Malhotra, Anju and Schuler, S.R. and Boender, C. (2002); *Measuring Women's Empowerment as a Variable in International Development,* Background Paper Prepared for the World Bank Workshop on Poverty and Gender; New Perspectives.
42. Ankerbo, Stine and Hoyda, Karina (2003); *"Education as a Means to Women's Empowerment"*, Opgave, Approaches to Development (U-Landshire) Aarthus University.

6
Research Methodology

While conducting the study, for the purpose of analysis, first of all we have considered all the households of each of the four selected villages in both the States taken together. The villages were chosen purposively on the basis of convenience, such as accessibility and communication, security, low expenditure, etc. Another important aspect that was kept in mind while determining the area of study was that each village must represent the State's dominant characteristics. It is then quite likely that each of the two villages in the States of Meghalaya and Tripura respectively bear the common features of the representative States.

In Kalitila in Tripura, there are 193 households and in Beltali, also in Tripura, there are 137 households i.e. there is a total of 330 households in the two selected villages of Tripura.

In the same way, there are 119 households in Ringkseh and 138 households in Kyton-u-Mon, both villages being in Meghalaya. In other words, there is a total of 257 households in the two selected villages of Meghalaya.

After listing the total 587 households from the two States, we have counted the male-headed and female-headed households. The ratio of male-headed and female-headed families is about 3 : 1 in the selected areas of Tripura and 1.6 : 1 in the selected areas of Meghalaya.

Although the State of Tripura is primarily patrilineal, yet we find that almost one-fourth of the selected families are headed by females. In the same way, contrary to the fact that the society of Meghalaya is commonly matrilineal, more than two-third of the families are run by males and only around one-third are headed by females. This indicates that the society of Meghalaya is also gradually shifting from its matrilineal backdrop and accepting the ways and traits of the dominant patrilineal society, thereby raising serious doubts about whether the dominance of the females is still prevailing or not.

We have stratified the families of the four villages in the two States according to the characteristics of caste, occupation and education, and finally we chose 204 households by stratified random sampling.

Using stratified random sampling in Beltali in Tripura, we have selected 36 out of the 110 male-headed households and 19 out of the 27 female-headed households. Again, using the same sampling in Kalitila, we randomly identified 36 out of the 154 male-headed households and 18 out of the 39 female-headed households. Adopting the same technique, in the village Ringkseh of Meghalaya, we randomly identified 25 out of the 73 male-headed households and 20 out of the 46 female-headed households as our sample population. In Kyton-u-Mon too, we selected at random 22 out of the 102 male-headed households and 28 out of the 36 female-headed households as our sample population.

The data required for the study have been collected from these selected households in the identified villages. Relevant data pertaining to family size, sex, education, caste, occupation, expenditure, income, etc., i.e. on social, cultural, economical, political, religious and psychological aspects have been collected. Subsequently, based on the available information, we tried to understand the process of empowerment by analyzing the data.

In addition, we have collected data from the counterparts of the heads of the same sets of households, for getting an alternative and comparative view about the different aspects related to the process of empowerment.

Moreover, we have also used different statistical techniques, whenever needed, for the sake of analytical exposition.

The standard sociological and anthropological methods of studying the social phenomena have been adhered to while conducting the study.

The schedule was finalized after pre-testing. The researcher himself conducted the interviews and the data collected from this source was supplemented and testified by other methods.

It was thought that to understand the prevailing social and political processes in the areas under study, it would be proper to use a combination of field study techniques, instead of relying upon a single method. Moreover, it is also very difficult to get a real insight into the problem by administering a well-prepared questionnaire alone. An important observation made in this context that is worthy of mention here is that the studied population is generally apprehensive while passing on some information, as they are guided by the fear that if they say something against the powerful section of the society, they may be unduly harassed. As such, due emphasis has been given on the observation techniques, case history and informal discussion. By staying with them for a long period, a close association could be developed with the concerned people. By this way more information was gathered.

Non-Participant Observation

Because of his past association with the State having stayed earlier in Agartala, the State capital, the researcher had substantial opportunity to observe the various aspects of the social and political life of the Panchayat members, especially that of the women living in the different parts of Tripura. Moreover, by observing them closely while they participated in Panchayat meetings or by paying informal visits to the houses of the women and attending their informal gatherings, the researcher could collect additional information. Insight was developed when the researcher participated actively in their informal decision-making process many a time because of his close knowledge of the area and his familiarity with the Panchayat members, especially the women of these areas.

Informal Discussions

Apart from the schedule and observation techniques, the researcher collected information through informal conversations with the selected households. By spending some time at the houses of the women and engaging them in informal chat sessions and thereby developing good relations with them, the researcher found for himself sufficient opportunity to have free and frank conversations, sometimes individually and sometimes in-groups. This technique proved to be very effective in understanding their attitude towards the existing social and political system. This method also helped in understanding the political dynamics of the area under study and revealed some 'inner stories' about the leaders.

Other Sources of Information

To understand the administrative aspects of the Survey Report, the District Gazetteers, the Census Handbook and Economic and Statistical Analysis, as well as the Government circulars issued from time to time were also consulted. Some of the information was also collected with the help of the Block and Panchayat officials.

At many places, it was necessary to rely upon the information supplied by the Block officials and any knowledgeable person in the locality. However, cross-checking was done to the extent possible, in order to avoid incorrect and biased information.

To avoid giving the interview the official touch, the time and place of interview was arranged according to the respondent's convenience. In some cases the interviews were also arranged at the site of their work. Only a few respondents, who were not easily approachable, were formally notified. In spite of all these precautions, some of them became too conscious and spoke in a guarded manner. However, in a few days time, most of them became free and frank in expressing their views. The field work process ended in six months.

Along with the interview rounds, the techniques of observation and informal conversation were also followed. The researcher went to the areas where the respondents lived and even attended their community meetings. Informal discussions were also arranged at the places of interviews. To give an informal and friendly touch to the entire field work, the researcher frequently shared breakfast, tea and a glass of water with the respondents. The researcher was of the view that it was necessary to observe their behaviour, habits, and attitudes closely to collect actual facts. The researcher used to maintain a personal diary and used to write his observations and personal impressions of the respondent Panchayat members, especially the women, during such interactions. This technique proved to be quite useful in gaining insight into their attitude.

Time Schedule

Though the tasks of interviewing the sample population and

collection of primary data were completed within six months, another one month was spent on follow-up to bridge any gaps in the data and ensure precision. Moreover, the scrutiny, transcription, tabulation and analysis of the data took some time.

Limitations of the Study

This study was confined to four villages in two districts, which cannot be claimed as a representative picture of the women's situation in the rural sector in Tripura and Meghalaya. It is, therefore, necessary to test the relevance of our findings in other geographical areas and villages, so that one can arrive at some generalization of women's empowerment patterns and processes.

The Reasons for Selecting the Two States of North-Eastern Region

In this sub-section we would like to mention the two main reasons that prompted us to select the two States of Meghalaya and Tripura as the area of study.

First and foremost, it has been observed that the 73rd Amendment is yet to be implemented in Meghalaya, while in Tripura, the above Amendment is already being implemented.

The notable contrast in the ethnic composition of the villages in Meghalaya and Tripura could be cited as the second reason for conducting the study work in these two States. For, while in Meghalaya, it was impossible to find a single multi-ethnic village, both the villages in Tripura were dominated by multi-ethnic characters. Hence, both the villages in Meghalaya consisted of the Khasi community exclusively and in Tripura, we found a multi-ethnic community in both the villages. Here there were a few Muslim families too. Moreover, while most of the villagers were occupied as agricultural labourers, a few also earned a livelihood from other occupations.

Other Relevant Informations

It may be informed that the data regarding the composition and structure of the households were collected through a pre-formatted schedule and the selected male household heads as well as female household heads have been interviewed in order to know their perception about the empowerment of women in the rural societies of the North-Eastern States.

So far as Meghalaya is concerned, a total of 95 households have been brought under the purview of our interview session in the two villages, the break-up of which is discussed hereafter. A limited number of 50 household heads in Kyton-u-Mon village were chosen as the sample population to be covered by the interview—28 out of 102 male household heads and 22 out of 36 female household heads in the village. Also, the heads of the families and their respective spouses from all the village households have been interviewed, so that a total of about 100 respondents from the village were interviewed. In Ringkseh village, out of the 119 households, a total of 45 household heads were chosen as the sample population. Precisely, as many as 25 out of 73 male household heads and 20 out of 45 female household heads have been chosen for the interview. Here too we have interviewed the spouses of the household heads also.

To understand the process of empowerment of women in rural areas, the main schedule covers different aspects of the social, cultural, political, environmental, economical, and religious life of the villagers.

In Tripura too, the data regarding the composition and structure of the households were collected in the same ways as mentioned for Meghalaya. In Beltali village in Tripura, where there were a total number of 137 households, we selected 36 out of 110 male household heads and 19 out of the 27 female household heads as our sample population. The household heads and their spouses as well have been interviewed by the study team, which implies that there were more than 100 respondents in Beltali. Again, in Kalitila, we randomly identified 36 out of the 154 male household heads and 18 out of the 39 female household heads and interviewed both the household heads and their spouses.

7
Data : Observations and Findings

(A) GENERAL PARTICULARS OF THE HOUSEHOLDS

Sex

The ratio of male to female is almost 1 : 1 in all the villages of Meghalaya, but in Tripura the ratio is 2 : 1, i.e., the number of males is more than the number of females in Tripura. In particular, out of the 109 households in Tripura, 72 are male-headed households and 37 are female-headed. Contrarily, in Meghalaya, where the family system is matrilineal, the number of males and females are almost equal. However, when we next take into consideration the Kyton-u-Mon village, we see that the number of females is more than the number of males (there are 22 males and 28 females out of 50 sample households—Table 7.1).

Again, if we consider the female-male ratio in these selected States after excluding the household heads and their respective counterparts (Table 7.2), then the ratio shows that in Meghalaya, there are 90 females per 100 males while in Tripura there are 88 females per 100 males.

On the other hand, if we include the heads of the households and their counterparts (Table 7.3), then the above ratio changes to 111 females per 100 males and 142 females per 100 males in Meghalaya and Tripura respectively.

Comparing Table 7.2 and Table 7.3, we could conclude that the former gives us better results in respect of the male-female ratio.

Table 7.1: Distribution of the Households by Sex of the Household Heads

State	Village	Sex		Total
(1)	(2)	(3)	(4)	(5)
		Male	Female	
Meghalaya	Ringkseh	25 (55.6)	20 (44.4)	45 (47.37)
	Kyton-u-Mon	22 (44)	28 (56)	50 (52.63)
	Total	47 (49.47)	48 (50.53)	95 (46.57)
Tripura	Beltali	36 (65.45)	19 (34.55)	55 (50.46)
	Kalitila	36 (66.67)	18 (33.33)	54 (49.54)
	Total	72 (66.06)	37 (33.94)	109 (53.43)
Grand Total		119 (58.33)	85 (41.67)	204 (100)

Table 7.2: Distribution by Sex excluding the Household Heads and their Counterparts

State	Village	Sex		Number of females/100 males	Total
		Male	Female		
Meghalaya	Ringkseh	60	72	120	132
	Kyton-u-Mon	92	66	71	158
	Total	152	138	90	290
Tripura	Beltali	69	54	78	123
	Kalitila	53	54	101	107
	Total	122	108	88	230
Grand Total		274	246	89	520

Caste

Caste is an important characteristic in rural areas. According to Ranganathan, caste has a vital role to play in the village system and in the traditional Panchayats in rural areas. But after democratic decentralization it has permeated to each and every aspect of rural life (Ranganathan, 1967: 267-276).

Table 7.3: Distribution by Sex including the Household Heads and their Counterparts

State	*Village*	*Sex*		*Number of females per 100 males*	*Total*
		Male	*Female*		
Meghalaya	Ringkseh	61	90	147	151
	Kyton-u-Mon	97	86	88	183
	Total	158	176	111	334
Tripura	Beltali	71	90	126	161
	Kalitila	54	88	162	142
	Total	125	178	142	303
Grand Total		283	354	125	637

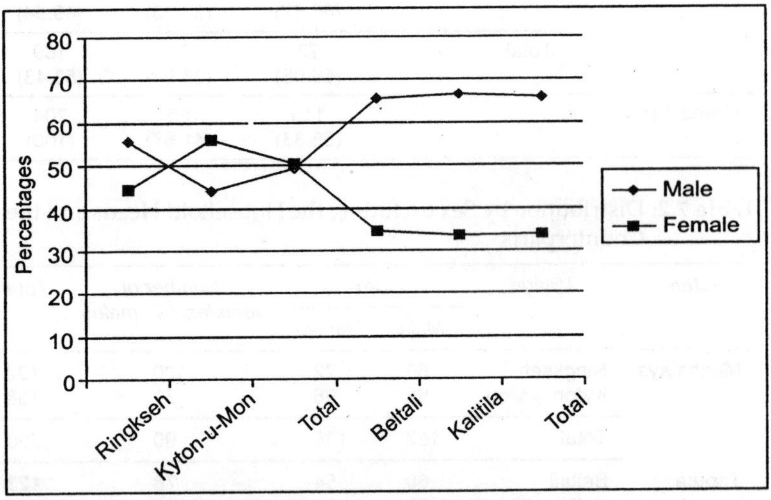

Fig. 7.1: Sex Distribution of the Household Heads

Srinivas explains how adult franchise has provided a new and important arena of activity for caste (Srinivas, 1962). He mentions three basic attributes of dominance of a caste, viz., numerical strength, control over land and ritual status. He adds that a caste which is endowed with all the three attributes of dominance is said to enjoy 'decisive dominance' in the village. He admits that 'decisive dominance' is not common and that the different elements of dominance more often remain distributed among the different caste-groups in the village. Thus a caste that is ritually high may be poor and lack numerical strength, while a populous caste may be poor and ritually low (Srinivas, 1959, 1-16).

According to Bhatt, as of now, there is a shift in the locus of power and influence from the ritually high-ranking castes to the numerically strong castes. (Bhatt, 1977, 297-319).

Table 7.4, which reflects the distribution of the village households by caste, reveals that in the studied villages of Tripura, there was only one family that belonged to the Muslim community. Neither of the villages in the State have any Christian family. Apart from this, in both the studied villages in the State, the Scheduled Castes (SC) of Hindu origin are more in number than the other castes and communities. However, in Kalitila, number-wise the SC families are followed by the general Hindu castes and the Other Backward Tribes (OBC) respectively. Another point to be noted in Table 7.4 under review is that while there are only 2 Scheduled Tribes (ST) families in Kalitila, they are more in number than any of the other castes in Beltali village of Tripura.

Coming next to the families in the studied villages of Meghalaya, we find that the ST families belonging to the Christian communities are more in number than the families of the other castes, in both the villages. Thus apart from the Christian ST families and 'Other Christians' (38 out of 45), who are in majority in Ringkseh village, there is only one Hindu SC family and one general ST family. 5 families belong to the 'Others' category. The Christian ST families constitute the majority in Kyton-u-Mon village where there is no trace of the others, except a handful (7 out of 50) belonging to the 'Others' category.

From the above findings we may conclude that whereas in Tripura, the maximum number of people belongs to the SC category under Hinduism, in Meghalaya, the Christian ST families dominate over the others with respect to numbers (Fig. 7.2 and 7.3).

Marital Status

Marriage is an important status-giving device (Bossard, 1944: 13). According to Kapadia (1966: 104), marriage is a source of personal gratification as well as the extension of social relations and responsibilities. In the context of empowerment, marital relationship helps one in understanding social roles; and through

Table 7.4: Distribution of the Households by Caste

State (1)	*Village* (2)	*Ethnic* (3)							*ST* (4)	*Total* (5)
		Hindu			*Muslim*	*Christian*		*Others/ NA*		
		General	*SC*	*OBC*		*ST*	*Others*			
Meghalaya	Ringkseh	0	1 (2.2)	0	0	37 (82.2)	1 (2.2)	5 (11.1)	1 (2.2)	45 (47.37)
	Kyton-u-Mon	0	0	0	0	43 (86)	0	7 (14)	0	50 (52.63)
	Total	0	1	0	0	80	1	12	1	95 (46.57)
Tripura	Beltali	13 (23.6)	15 (27.3)	7 (12.7)	0	0	0	1 (1.8)	19 (34.5)	55 (50.46)
	Kalitila	14 (25.9)	28 (51.9)	9 (16.7)	1 (1.9)	0	0	0	2 (3.7)	54 (49.54)
	Total	27	43	16	1	0	0	1	21	109 (53.43)

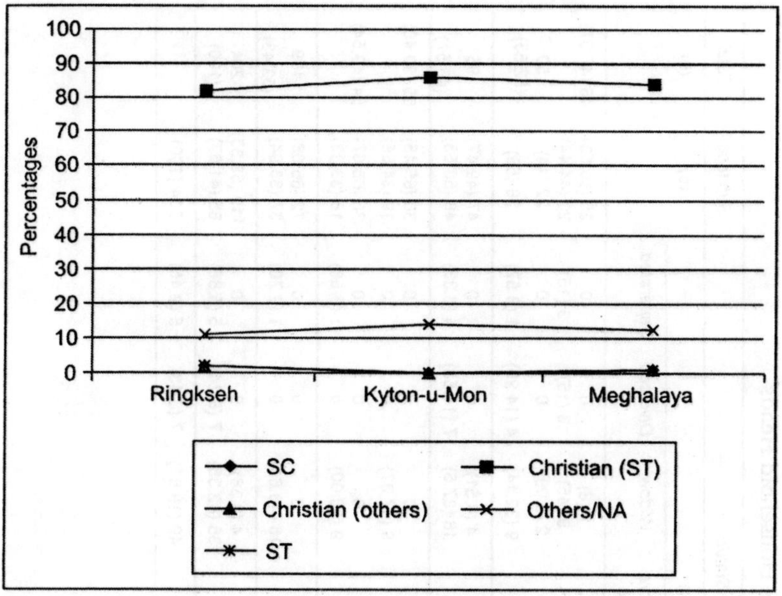

Fig. 7.2: Distribution of the Households by Caste in Meghalaya

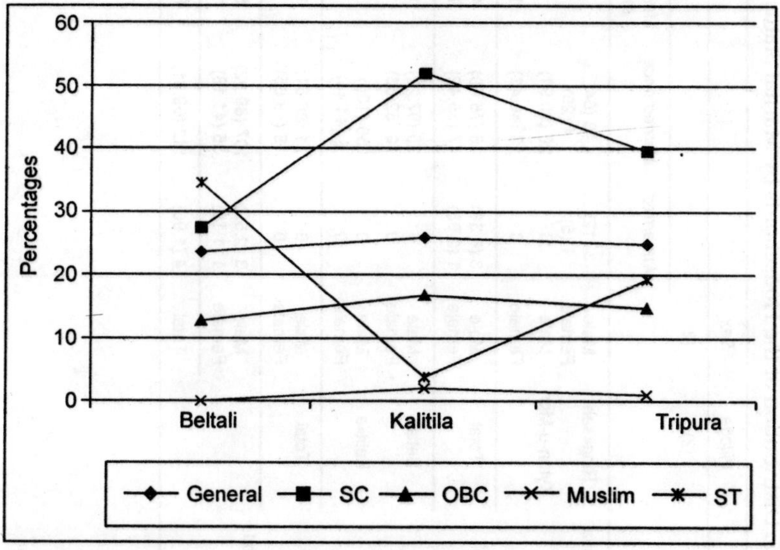

Fig. 7.3: Distribution of the Households by Caste in Tripura

Table 7.5: Distribution of the Households by Marital Status of the Household Heads

State	Village	Sex	Marital Status						Sub total	Total
(1)	(2)	(3)	(4)						(5)	(6)
			Unmarried	Married once	Married more than once	Widow	Divorced	Separated		
Meghalaya	Ringkseh	Male	3 (12)	16 (64)	4 (16)	2 (8)	0	0	25 (55.56)	45 (47.37)
		Female	1 (5)	4 (20)	0	9 (45)	3 (15)	3 (15)	20 (44.44)	
	Kyton-u-Mon	Male	0	20 (90.91)	0	2 (9.09)	0	0	22 (44)	50 (52.63)
		Female	0	13 (46.43)	1 (3.57)	9 (32.14)	4 (14.29)	1 (3.57)	28 (56)	
	Total	Male	3 (6.38)	36 (76.60)	4 (8.51)	4 (8.51)	0	0	47 (49.47)	95 (46.57)
		Female	1 (2.08)	17 (35.42)	1 (2.08)	18 (37.5)	7 (14.58)	4 (8.33)	48 (50.53)	
Tripura	Beltali	Male	0	35 (97.22)	1 (2.78)	0	0	0	36 (65.45)	55 (50.46)
		Female	0	10 (52.63)	0	9 (47.37)	0	0	19 (34.55)	
	Kalitila	Male	0	36 (100)	0	0	0	0	36 (66.67)	54 (49.54)
		Female	0	8 (44.44)	0	9 (50.00)	0	1 (5.56)	18 (33.33)	
	Total	Male	0	71 (98.61)	1 (1.39)	0	0	0	72 (66.06)	109 (53.43)
		Female	0	18 (48.65)	0	18 (48.65)	0	1 (2.70)	37 (33.94)	
Grand Total		Male	3 (2.52)	107 (89.92)	5 (4.20)	4 (3.36)	0	0	119 (58.33)	204 (100)
		Female	1 (1.18)	35 (41.18)	1 (1.18)	36 (42.35)	7 (8.24)	5 (5.88)	85 (41.67)	
		Total	4 (1.96)	142 (69.61)	6 (2.94)	40 (19.61)	7 (3.43)	5 (2.45)	204 (100)	

a set of affinal relations, it enlarges his/her support-syndrome, which may empower him/her.

Table 7.5 reflects the distribution of the village households by the marital status of the household heads. According to it, 12 per cent of the males who are household heads and 5 per cent of the females who are household heads in the villages in Meghalaya are 'Unmarried'. It reveals that the 'Married Once' category of household heads dominate over all the other categories shown in the Table, like 'Married more than Once', 'Widow', and 'Divorced', including the 'Unmarried' categories of males and females. It also gets noticed that in the female-headed households, there is a significant number of women in the 'Widow' and 'Divorced' categories. Thus the percentages for widows in Ringkseh and Kyton-u-Mon are 45 per cent and 32.14 per cent respectively.

So far as the picture in the studied villages of Tripura is concerned, the Table 7.5 makes it clear that there is only 1 male among all the male and female-headed families in both the villages, who has married more than once. While there are none among the interviewed males and females who is unmarried, the sample population has a maximum number in the 'Married Once' category, irrespective of the sex of the household heads. However, a significant number of females who are family heads are widows. As per Table 7.5 under consideration, 47.37 per cent and 50 per cent of the female family heads in Beltali and Kalitila villages respectively are widows. Interestingly, none of the males who are family heads are widowers in either of the villages.

A contrasting character of the studied population in the villages of Meghalaya and Tripura that gets revealed is that while in Meghalaya, we find one woman who married more than once, there is none to be found in this category among the women in Tripura. However, there is one man in the sample population from this State who is married more than once Figs. 7.4 and 7.5).

Family Type

An attempt has been made by the study team to determine the village households on the basis of family types, whether the different households are nuclear or joint. As we are aware, the nuclear family type is rapidly gaining grounds over the joint family type in most parts of our country. Table 7.6 below will help us

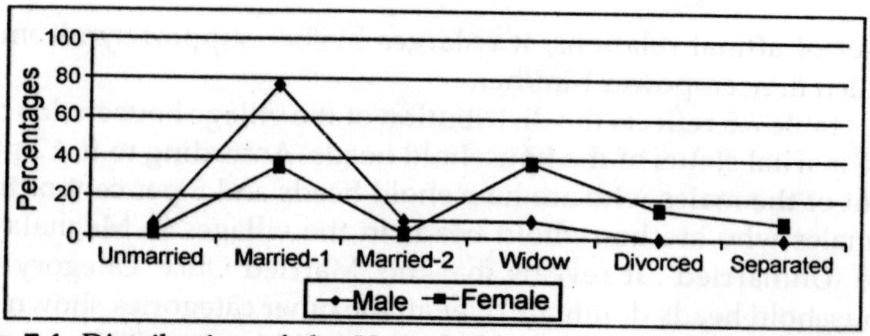

Fig. 7.4: Distribution of the Household Heads by Marital Status in Meghalaya

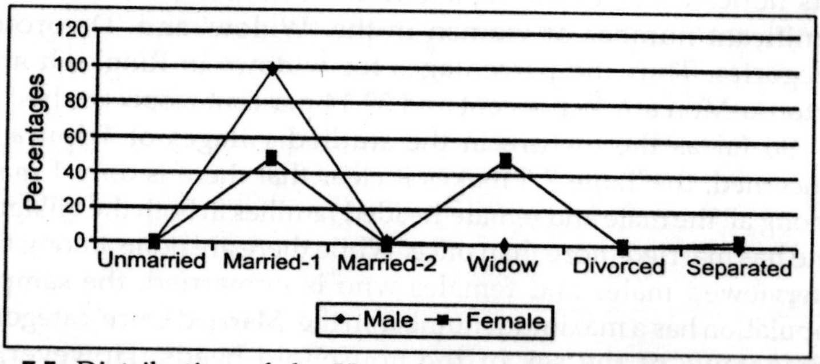

Fig. 7.5: Distribution of the Household Heads by Marital Status in Tripura

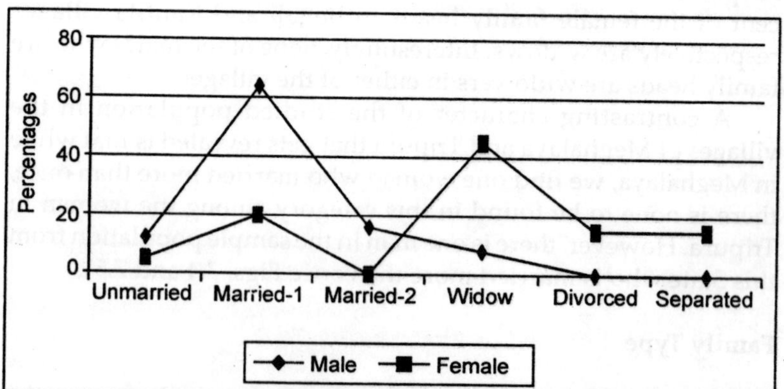

Fig. 7.6: Distribution of the Household Heads by Marital Status in Ringkseh

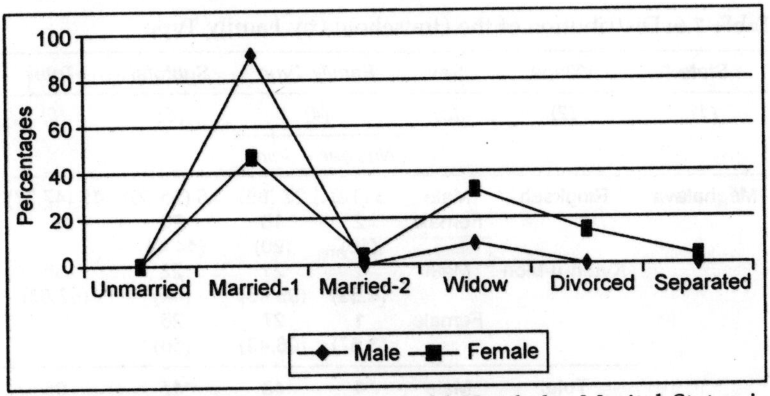

Fig. 7.7: Distribution of the Household Heads by Marital Status in Kyton-u-Mon

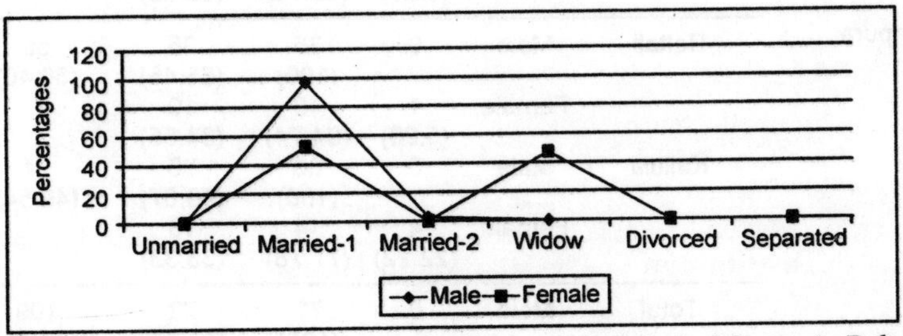

Fig. 7.8: Distribution of the Household Heads by Marital Status in Beltali

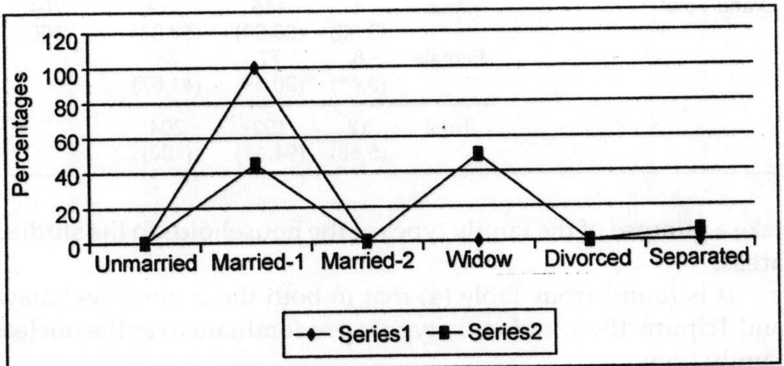

Fig. 7.9: Distribution of the Household Heads by Marital Status in Kalitila

Table 7.6: Distribution of the Households by Family Type

State	*Village*	*Sex*	*Family Type*		*Subtotal*	*Total*
(1)	*(2)*	*(3)*	*(4)*		*(5)*	*(6)*
			Nuclear	*Joint*		
Meghalaya	Ringkseh	Male	3 (12)	22 (88)	25 (55.56)	45 (47.37)
		Female	2 (10)	18 (90)	20 (44.44)	
	Kyton-u-Mon	Male	1 (4.55)	21 (95.45)	22 (44)	50 (52.63)
		Female	1 (3.57)	27 (96.43)	28 (56)	
	Total	Male	4 (8.51)	43 (91.49)	47 (49.47)	95 (46.57)
		Female	3 (6.25)	45 (93.75)	48 (50.53)	
Tripura	Beltali	Male	0	36 (100)	36 (65.45)	55 (50.46)
		Female	1 (5.26)	18 (94.74)	19 (34.55)	
	Kalitila	Male	0	36 (100)	36 (66.67)	54 (49.54)
		Female	4 (22.22)	14 (77.78)	18 (33.33)	
	Total	Male	0	72 (100)	72 (66.06)	109 (53.43)
		Female	5 (13.51)	32 (86.49)	37 (33.94)	
Grand Total		Male	4 (3.36)	115 (96.64)	119 (58.33)	204 (100)
		Female	8 (9.41)	77 (90.59)	85 (41.67)	
		Total	12 (5.88)	192 (94.12)	204 (100)	

take a glimpse of the family types of the households in the studied areas.

It is found from Table (4) that in both the states, Meghalaya and Tripura, the joint family type is predominant over the nuclear family type.

It is also noticed that there are no nuclear male-headed families present in either Beltali or Kalitila in Tripura. However, the two villages taken together, there are 5 nuclear type families among the 37 female-headed families.

In Meghalaya, on the other hand, there are a total of 4 nuclear type male-headed families and 3 nuclear type female-headed families.

If we consider both the States together, 94.12 per cent of the total households surveyed adhere to the joint family system and only 5.88 per cent have opted for the nuclear family type. To be precise, out of the total 204 households brought under the purview of this study, 192 households follow the joint family type and only 12 households have identified themselves as nuclear families (Figs. 7.10 and 7.11).

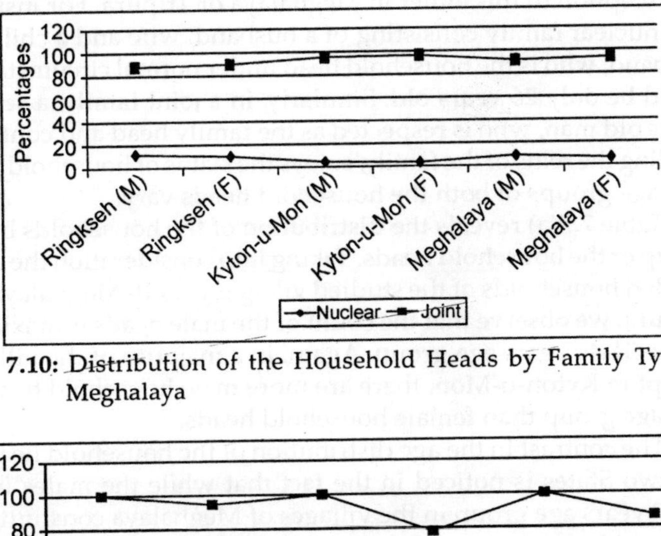

Fig. 7.10: Distribution of the Household Heads by Family Type in Meghalaya

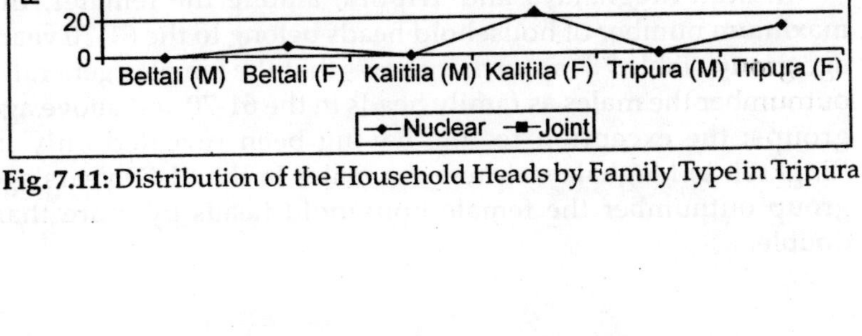

Fig. 7.11: Distribution of the Household Heads by Family Type in Tripura

Age Group

Society has largely been male dominated and so it is mainly a male person who is the unconditional head of a household. However, with times, as the social structure too is changing significantly, today there are quite a few female household heads too. Similarly, given the varying family situations, the ages of all the household heads, irrespective of sex, will obviously be different and a number of factors contribute towards determining their age groups. If for some reasons, a 30-year old man is required to shoulder family responsibilities as household head at a comparatively young age, for obvious reasons, an old and feeble man of 70 years also has to continue taking up the responsibilities of his family. And there is no exception to this either in Meghalaya or Tripura. For instance, in a nuclear family consisting of a husband, wife and a child, the husband, who is the household head under normal circumstances, could be only 26 years old. Similarly, in a joint family, a seventy years old man, who is respected as the family head and continues holding the reins of the family, enjoys the status of household head. The age groups of both the household heads vary.

Table 7.7(a) reveals the distribution of the households by age group of the household heads. Taking into consideration the male-headed households of the studied villages in both Meghalaya and Tripura, we observe that the count of the male heads is maximum in the 31-40 years age group. Again, in a majority of the villages, except in Kyton-u-Mon, there are more male household heads in this age group than female household heads.

The contrast in the age distribution of the household heads in the two States is noticed in the fact that while the males in the 61-70 years age group in the villages of Meghalaya constitute the second biggest group of male household heads, in Tripura the males in the 41-50 years could stake that claim.

In both Meghalaya and Tripura, among the females, the maximum number of household heads belong to the 61-70 years age group. Table 7.7(a) further shows that the females generally outnumber the males as family heads in the 61-70 and above age groups; the exception to this having been revealed only in Ringkseh in Meghalaya where the males in the 61-70 years age group outnumber the female household heads by more than double.

Table 7.7(a): Distribution of the Households by Age Groups of the Household Heads

State (1)	Village (2)	Sex (3)	Age group (4)						Subtotal (5)	Total (6)
			20-30	31-40	41-50	51-60	61-70	>70		
Meghalaya	Ringkseh	Male	1 (4)	7 (28)	3 (12)	5 (20)	9 (36)	0	25 (55.56)	45 (47.37)
		Female	1 (5)	3 (15)	3 (15)	5 (25)	4 (20)	4 (20)	20 (44.44)	
	Kyton-u-Mon	Male	3 (13.64)	5 (22.73)	5 (22.73)	5 (22.73)	2(9.09)	2 (9.09)	22 (44)	50 (52.63)
		Female	2 (7.14)	6 (21.43)	6 (21.43)	5 (17.86)	7 (25)	2 (7.14)	28 (56)	
	Total	Male	4 (8.51)	12 (25.53)	8 (17.02)	10 (21.28)	11 (23.40)	2 (4.26)	47 (49.47)	95 (46.57)
		Female	3 (6.25)	9 (18.75)	9 (18.75)	10 (20.83)	11 (22.92)	6 (12.5)	48 (50.53)	
Tripura	Beltali	Male	3 (8.33)	9 (25)	9 (25)	7 (19.44)	4 (11.11)	4 (11.11)	36 (65.45)	55 (50.46)
		Female	0	0	4 (21.05)	6 (31.58)	7 (36.84)	2 (10.53)	19 (34.55)	
	Kalitila	Male	3 (8.33)	15 (41.67)	8 (22.22)	7 (19.44)	3 (8.33)	0	36 (66.67)	54 (49.54)
		Female	1 (5.56)	2 (11.11)	3 (16.67)	4 (22.22)	4 (22.22)	4 (22.22)	18 (33.33)	
	Total	Male	6 (8.33)	24 (33.33)	17 (23.61)	14 (19.44)	7 (9.72)	4 (5.56)	72 (66.06)	109 (53.43)
		Female	1 (2.70)	2 (5.41)	7 (18.92)	10 (27.03)	11 (29.73)	6 (16.22)	37 (33.94)	
Grand Total		Male	10 (8.40)	36 (30.25)	25 (21.01)	24 (20.17)	18 (15.13)	6 (5.04)	119 (58.33)	204 (100)
		Female	4 (4.71)	11 (12.94)	16 (18.82)	20 (23.53)	22 (25.88)	12 (14.12)	85 (41.67)	
		Total	14 (6.86)	47 (23.04)	41 (20.10)	44 (21.57)	40 (19.61)	18 (8.82)	204 (100)	

Table 7.7(b): Distribution of the Households by Age Groups of the Counterparts of the Household Heads

State (1)	Village (2)	Sex (3)	Age group (4)						Sub-total (5)	Total (6)
			20-30	31-40	41-50	51-60	61-70	>70		
Meghalaya	Ringkseh	Male	9	4	3	0	0	0	16	
		Female	2	6	3	6	2	0	19	
	Kyton-u-Mon	Male	12	4	2	0	1	1	20	
		Female	6	7	4	2	1	1	21	
	Total	Male	21	8	5	0	1	1	36	
		Female	8	13	7	8	3	1	40	
Tripura	Beltali	Male	8	7	1	1	0	0	17	
		Female	10	10	6	7	2	1	36	
	Kalitila	Male	4	7	3	0	0	0	14	
		Female	17	8	5	5	1	0	36	
	Total	Male	12	14	4	1	0	0	31	
		Female	27	18	11	12	3	1	72	
Grand Total		Male	33	22	9	1	1	1	67	
		Female	35	31	18	20	6	2	112	
		Total	68	53	27	21	7	3	179	

From the above, we could safely say that the male heads are significantly more in number in the lower age group of 31-40 years, whereas the number of female heads is slightly more in the higher

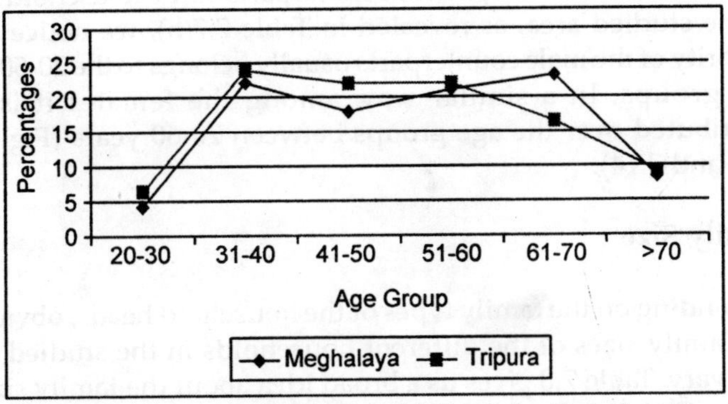

Fig. 7.12: Distribution of the Household Heads by their Age Groups in Meghalaya and Tripura

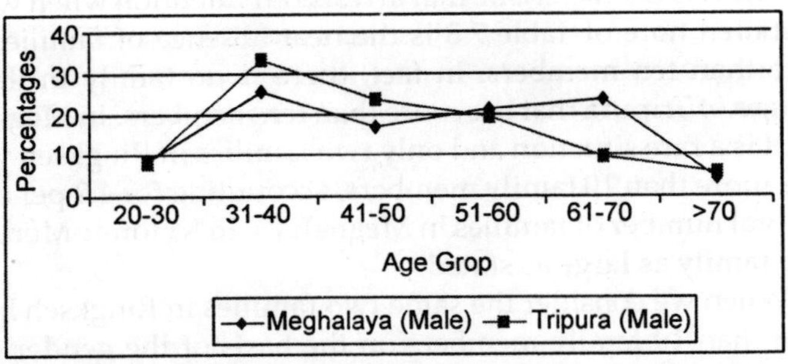

Fig. 7.13: Distribution of the Male-Headed Household Heads by their Age Groups in Meghalaya and Tripura

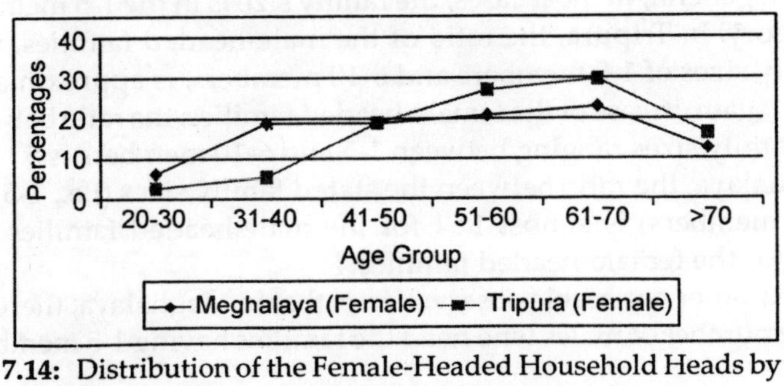

Fig. 7.14: Distribution of the Female-Headed Household Heads by their Age Groups in Meghalaya and Tripura

age group (61-70 years). There are only a few heads who are below 31 years or above 70 years. Most of the heads above 70 years are females.

In pursuance of the findings of the study, when we next shift our attention to the respective counterparts of the household heads in the studied area, as revealed in Table 7.7(b), we notice that a majority of the male counterparts usually belongs to the 20-50 years age groups. In a similar way, among the females it is well distributed over the age groups between 20-60 years (Fig. 7.12, 7.13 and 7.14).

Family Size

Depending on the family types of the household heads, obviously, the family sizes of the different households in the studied areas will vary. Table 7.8 gives us a broad idea about the family sizes of the households in the four studied villages in Meghalaya and Tripura.

The one characteristic that arrests our attention when we take a detailed note of Table 7.8 is the near absence of families with more than ten members. In fact, there is no family in the two villages of Tripura that has more than ten members. In Meghalaya too, it is a rare situation and only two families in Ringkseh village have more than 10 family members, accounting for 4.2 per cent of the total number of families in Meghalaya. In Kyton-u-Mon, there is no family as large as stated.

When we consider the same two families in Ringkseh having more than 10 family members on the basis of the gender of the household heads, we see that one of the families is male-headed and the other is female-headed.

In general, in most cases, the family size is in the 1-5 members category. In Tripura, the ratio of the male-headed families, with family sizes of 1-5 members and 6-10 members, is approximately 6 : 1. Again, in case of the female-headed families, the ratio between the family sizes ranging between 1-5 and 6-10 members is 5 : 1. In Meghalaya, the ratio between the stated family sizes (i.e., 1-5 and 6-10 members) is almost 1 : 1 for the male-headed families and 2 : 1 for the female-headed families.

Another noticeable observation is that in Meghalaya, there are more number of males who head the families having 1-5 members,

Table 7.8: Distribution of the Households by Family Size

State (1)	*Village (2)*	*Literacy Status (3)*	*Family Size* *Male (4)*			*Sub-total*	*Female (5)*			*Sub-Total*	*Total (6)*
			1-5	*6-10*	*>10*		*1-5*	*6-10*	*>10*		
Meghalaya	Ringkseh	Illiterate	0	1(4)	0	25	1(5)	1(5)	0	20 (44.44)	45 47.37)
		<Madhyamik	9(36)	5(20)	1(4)	(55.56)	11(55)	3(15)	1(5)		
		>Madhyamik	4(16)	5(20)	0		1(5)	2(10)	0		
	Kyton-u-Mon	Illiterate	1(4.5)	5(22.7)	0	22	11(39.3)	5(17.9)	0	28	50
		<Madhyamik	4(18.2)	7(31.8)	0	(44)	4(14.3)	4(14.3)	0	(56)	(52.63)
		>Madhyamik	5(22.7)	0	0		3(10.7)	1(3.6)	0		
	Total	Illiterate	1(2.1)	6(12.8)	0	47	12(25)	6(12.5)	0	48	95
		<Madhyamik	13(27.7)	12(25.5)	1(2.1)	(49.47)	15(31.25)	7(14.6)	1(2.1)	(50.53)	(46.57)
		>Madhyamik	9(19.1)	5(10.6)	0		4(8.3)	3(6.25)	0		
Tripura	Beltali	Illiterate	5(13.9)	0	0	36	9(47.4)	4(21.1)	0	19	55
		<Madhyamik	23(63.9)	5(13.9)	0	(65.45)	5(26.3)	1(5.3)	0	(34.55)	(50.46)
		>Madhyamik	2(5.6)	1(2.8)	0		0	0	0		
	Kalitila	Illiterate	3(8.3)	2(5.6)	0	36	9(50)	0	0	18	54
		<Madhyamik	20(55.6)	2(5.6)	0	(66.67)	8(44.4)	1(5.6)	0	(33.33)	(49.54)
		>Madhyamik	8(22.2)	1(2.8)	0		0	0	0		
	Total	Illiterate	8(11.1)	2(2.8)	0	72	18(48.6)	4(10.8)	0	37	109
		<Madhyamik	43(59.7)	7(9.7)	0	(66.06)	13(35.1)	2(5.4)	0	(33.94)	(53.43)
		>Madhyamik	10(13.9)	2(2.8)	0		0	0	0		
Grand Total			84 (70.59)	34 (28.57)	1 (0.8)	119 (58.33)	62 (72.9)	22 (25.9)	1 (1.2)	85 (41.67)	204 (100)

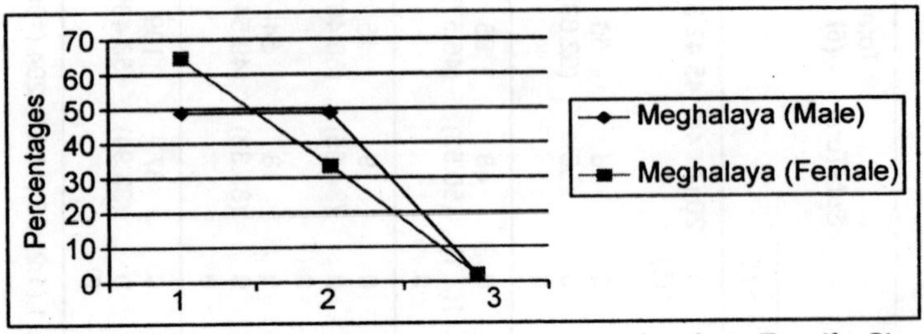

Fig. 7.15: Distribution of the Household Heads by their Family Size in Meghalaya

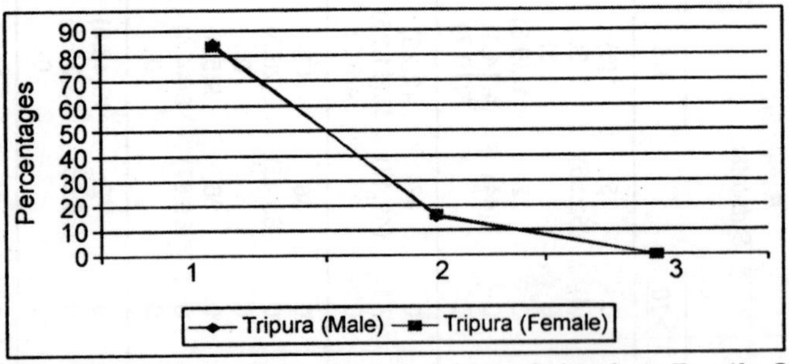

Fig. 7.16: Distribution of the Household Heads by their Family Size in Tripura

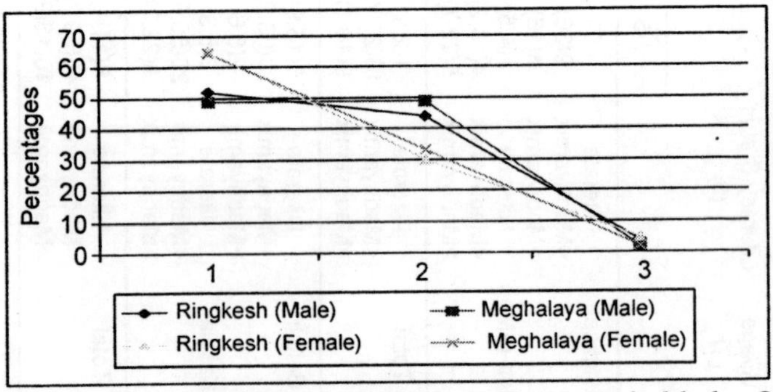

Fig. 7.17: Comparing the Family Sizes of the Households by Sex in Ringkseh with that of Meghalaya

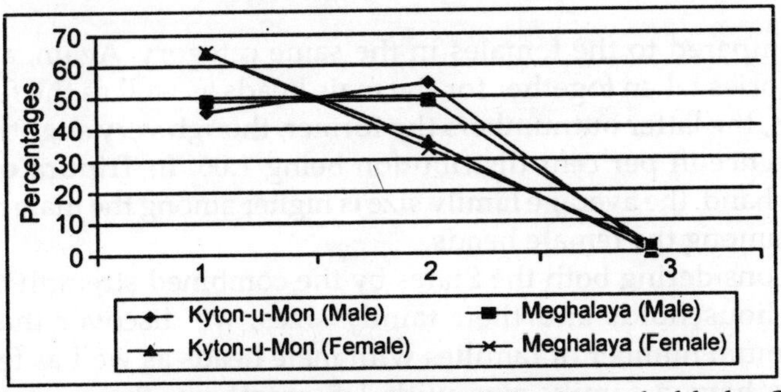

Fig. 7.18: Comparing the Family Sizes of the Households by Sex in Kyton-u-Mon with that of Meghalaya

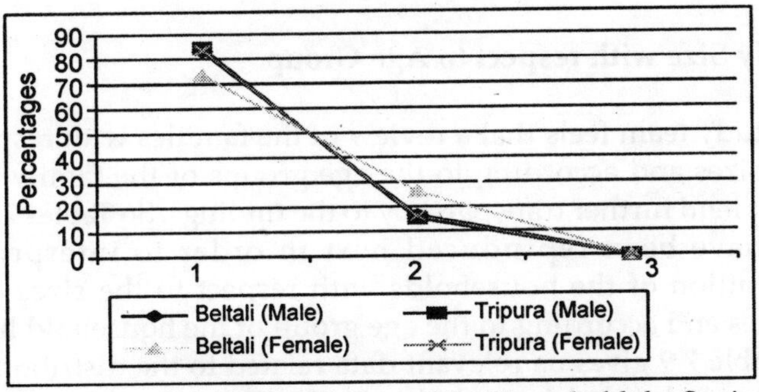

Fig. 7.19: Comparing the Family Sizes of the Households by Sex in Beltali with that of Tripura

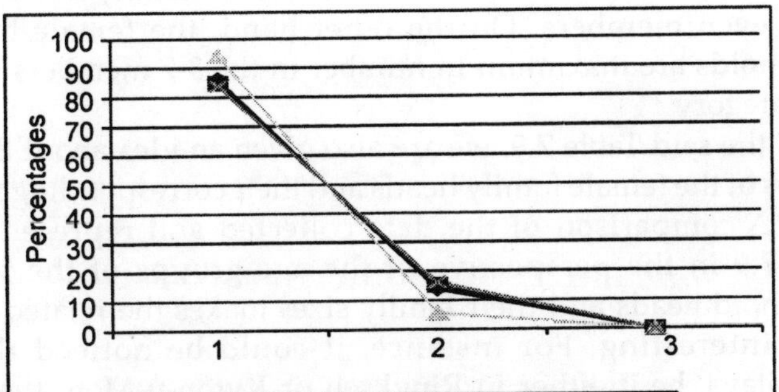

1 → Family size from 1 to 5; 2→Family sizes from 5 to 10; 3→Family sizes more than 10

Fig. 7.20: Comparing the Family Sizes of the Households by Sex in Kalitila with that of Tripura

as compared to the females in the same category. Again, all the categories taken together for the male heads as well as the female heads, the latter outnumbers the former, though very slightly, the difference in per cent distribution being 1.06. In Tripura on the other hand, the average family size is higher among the male heads than among the female heads.

Considering both the States by the combined strength of the total households and their family sizes, we discover that the maximum number of families with male heads as well as female heads have a family size with 1-5 members, the percentage distribution of the families being 70.59 per cent for the males and 72.94 per cent for the females (Fig 7.15 to 7.20).

Family Size with respect to Age Group

The study team feels that a review of the families with respect to their sizes and according to the age groups of the family heads would lend further transparency to the findings. So Tables 7.9 and 7.10 have been reproduced next in order to interpret the distribution of the households with respect to the sizes of the families and according to the age group of the household heads.

Table 7.9 gives us relevant data related to the distribution of the female-headed households by family size. An analysis of Table 7.9 reveals that in both Meghalaya and Tripura, a very small number of female-headed households have a family size of more than seven members. On the other hand, the female-headed households are maximum in number in the 3-7 members family size category.

In the said Table 7.9, we are also given an idea about the age groups of the female family heads and their corresponding family sizes. A comparison of the data collected and represented in Table 7.9 in the perspective of the age groups of the female household heads and their family sizes makes the related study more interesting. For instance, it could be noticed that in Meghalaya, be it either in Ringkseh or Kyton-u-Mon, there are three female-headed families each, with a family size of 1-2 member/s, where the female heads are over 60 years old. Again, whereas in Ringkseh, the females in the 41-60 years age group who head a 3-7 family size are maximum in number, in Kyton-u-Mon, females heading a 3-7 family size may likewise be

Table 7.9: Distribution of the Female-Headed Households by Family Size

State	*Village*	*Age*	*Family Size*			*Total*	*BPL Percentage*
			1-2	3-7	> 7		
Meghalaya	Ringkseh	20-40	0	3	1	20	15
		41-60	1	7	0		
		>60	3	4	1		
	Kyton-u-Mon	20-40	0	8	0	28	17.86
		41-60	5	5	1		
		>60	3	5	1		
	Total		12	32	4	48	16.67
Tripura	Beltali	20-40	0	0	0	19	15.79
		41-60	3	6	1		
		>60	1	8	0		
	Kalitila	20-40	0	3	0	18	22.22
		41-60	2	5	0		
		>60	4	4	0		
	Total		10	26	1	37	18.92
Grand Total			22	58	5	85	17.65

Table 7.10: Distribution of the Male-Headed Households by Family Size

State	*Village*	*Age*	*Family Size*			*Total*	*BPL Percentage*
			1-2	*3-7*	*> 7*		
Meghalaya	Ringkseh	20-40	1	7	1	25	8
		41-60	2	4	2		
		>60	2	5	1		
	Kyton-u-Mon	20-40	0	8	0	22	4.55
		41-60	1	7	2		
		>60	0	4	0		
	Total		6	35	6	47	6.38
Tripura	Beltali	20-40	2	10	0	36	13.89
		41-60	2	14	0		
		>60	3	5	0		
	Kalitila	20-40	0	11	1	36	8.33
		41-60	6	13	1		
		>60	2	2	0		
	Total		15	55	2	72	11.11
Grand Total			21	90	8	119	9.24

maximum in number, but the ages of the female heads ranges in the 21-40 years age group.

When we turn our attention to Tripura next, we observe that in both the villages taken together, there are more numbers of females heading a 3-7 member family size. Now, in so far as their ages are concerned, in both Beltali and Kalitila, the maximum number of the female heads having a 3-7 family size belong to the 41-60 years age group.

We are next going to consider the case of the male-headed families in the studied villages, according to the age groups of the household heads and family sizes, on the basis of the data in Table 7.10.

Overall, in both Meghalaya and Tripura, a maximum number of the male family heads have a family size of 3-7 members. However, considering the State based village-wise age-group distribution of the male family heads, first in Meghalaya, we see that in Ringkseh, the ages of a maximum number of the males (7) heading a family size of 3-7 members are in the 20-40 age group. Again, as per the available data, there is 1 male head in Ringkseh having a family size of 1-2 members and teaming up in the 20-40 years age group.

We derive a similar picture in Kyton-u-Mon too. We see that in Kyton-u-Mon, the number of males (8) in the 20-40 age group/

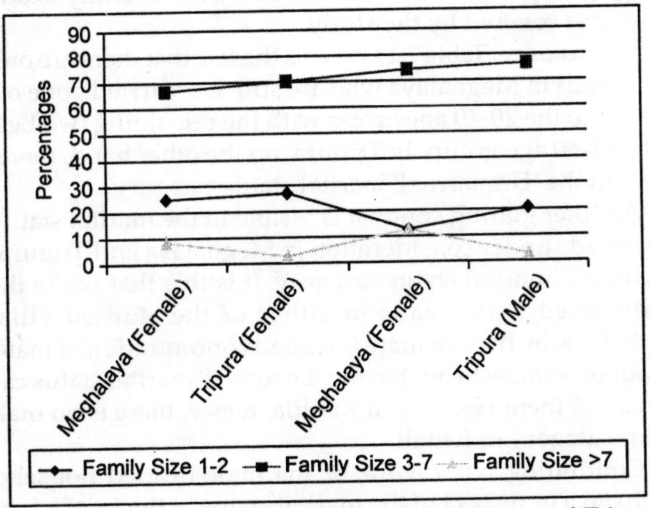

Fig. 7.21: Comparison of the Family Sizes in Meghalaya and Tripura

3-7 members range is only slightly more than the male heads (7) in the 40-60 age group/3-7 members range.

In the villages of Tripura, however, the scene is a little different as although a maximum number of males in both the sample villages head family units consisting of 3-7 members, those in the 41-60 years age group are maximum in number, unlike in Meghalaya where the males in the 20-40 age group are a single majority. However, the distribution of the male heads in the 20-40 age groups with 3-7 family members is also not quite insignificant in either of the two villages, i.e., Beltali (10) and Kalitila (11) Fig. 7.21.

Marital Status with respect to Age Group

In the context of the analytical discussion in progress, it would be pertinent to next study the marital status of the respondents with respect to age-group. Table 7.11 and Table 7.12, which have been reproduced hereafter, throw light on the distribution of the male-headed and female-headed households in Meghalaya and Tripura by the marital status of the family heads.

We have, first of all, made an effort to analyze the data made available in Table 7.11, by bringing out the contrasts in respect of the age groups and marital status of the male family heads in the two States covered by the study.

For instance, Table 7.11 reveals the fact that there are only three male heads in Meghalaya who are still 'Unmarried', one of whom belongs to the 20-40 age group with the remaining two belonging to the 41-60 age group. In Tripura, on the other hand, there are no males in the 'Unmarried' marital status category.

Another glaring contrast is visible in the marital status of the male heads under consideration in Meghalaya and Tripura, in the 'Divorced" marital status category. It is this that while there are no divorced male heads in either of the studied villages in Meghalaya, in Tripura there is a good concentration of male heads (33 out of 36 male heads) in the 'Divorced' marital status category, with all of them residing in Kalitila; hence, there is no male head in this category in Beltali.

Continuing our review of the male-headed households in Meghalaya in respect of the marital status of the family heads, we decipher that a maximum number of the males (36 out of 47 male

Table 7.11: Distribution of the Male-Headed Households by Marital Status of the Head of the Family

State	*Village*	*Age Group*	*Marital Status*					*Total*
			Unmarried	*Widow(er)*	*Divorced*	*Married once*	*Married more than once*	
Meghalaya	Ringkseh	20-40	1	0	0	7	0	25
		41-60	2	0	0	4	2	
		>60	0	2	0	5	2	
	Kyton-u-Mon	20-40	0	0	0	8	0	22
		41-60	0	0	0	10	0	
		>60	0	0	0	2	2	
	Total		3	2	0	36	6	47
Tripura	Beltali	20-40	0	0	0	12	0	36
		41-60	0	0	0	16	0	
		>60	0	0	0	7	1	
	Kalitila	20-40	0	0	18	0	0	36
		41-60	0	0	15	0	0	
		>60	0	0	3	0	0	
	Total		0	0	36	35	1	72
Grand Total			3	2	36	71	7	119

Table 7.12: Distribution of the Female-Headed Households by Marital Status of the Head of the Family

State	Village	Age Group	Marital Status						Total
			Unmarried	Widow	Divorced	Married One	Separated	Married twice	
Meghalaya	Ringkseh	20-40	1	0	1	1	1	0	20
		41-60	0	4	2	1	1	0	
		>60	0	5	0	2	1	0	
	Kyton-u-Mon	20-40	0	2	1	4	0	1	28
		41-60	0	5	2	3	1	0	
		>60	0	2	1	6	0	0	
Total			1	18	7	17	4	1	48
Tripura	Beltali	20-40	0	0	0	0	0	0	19
		41-60	0	5	0	5	0	0	
		>60	0	4	0	5	0	0	
	Kalitila	20-40	0	1	0	2	0	0	18
		41-60	0	3	0	3	1	0	
		>60	0	5	0	3	0	0	
	Total		0	18	0	18	1	0	37
Grand Total			1	36	7	35	5	1	85

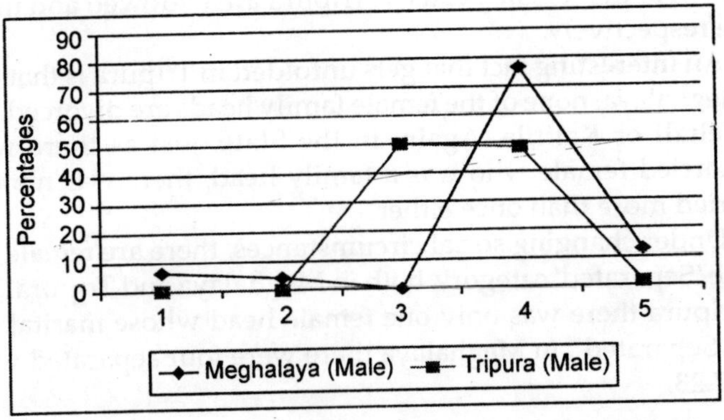

Fig. 7.22: Distribution of Male Headed Households by Marital Status in Meghalaya and Tripura

household heads) in the two studied villages are 'Married Once' only. However, the presence of male family heads who are married more than once is also not very hard to find in the two villages, with Ringkteh reporting four male heads who are 'More than Once Married' and Kyton-u-Mon reporting two 'More than Once Married' male heads.

In Tripura, the marital status of most of the male heads (33) could be identified as 'Once Married', while there are none in the 'Widow(er)' category (Figure 7.22).

Table 7.12 reveals the distribution of the female-headed households in the studied villages in Meghalaya and Tripura by the marital status of the head of the family.

In Meghalaya, the number-wise distribution of the female family heads in decreasing order goes thus: Widow—18, Married Once—17, Divorced—7, Separated—4 and More Twice—1. The two villages in the State taken separately, there are 5 widows each in Ringkseh and Kytun-o-Mon, who belong to the above 60 years age group and 41-60 years age group respectively. Only one woman in Kyton-u-Mon is reportedly married twice. Again, there are 2 widowed women in the 20-40 years age groups in Kytun-u-Mon village.

Percent-wise, 37.5 per cent of the female family heads in Meghalaya are widowed, 35.41 per cent are 'Married Once' and 14.58 per cent are 'Divorced.' Similarly, 42.35 per cent and 41.18

per cent of the female heads in Tripura are widowed and married once respectively.

An interesting fact that gets unfolded in Tripura is that unlike in Meghalaya, none of the female family heads are divorced, either in Beltali or Kalitila. Again, in the State, just as there was no unmarried female who was a family head, there was none who married more than once either.

Under changing social circumstances, there are female heads in the 'Separated' category, both in Meghalaya and Tripura. While in Tripura there was only one female head whose marital status was 'Separated', in Meghalaya there were four separated women Fig. 7.23.

Preference for Children by Sex

One of the many interpretations as available in The Webster's New World Dictionary defines a family as 'a social unit consisting of the parents and their children'. So it is quite likely that the households in the study areas in the two States consisted of a good number of children. However, we believe that the count of children in the households did not have any relevance to the study. Instead, it would be justified if we could get the parents to disclose their preference for male and female children. In other words, did the parents, by their status as family heads, have any preference about the sex of their children? We have made an attempt to collect

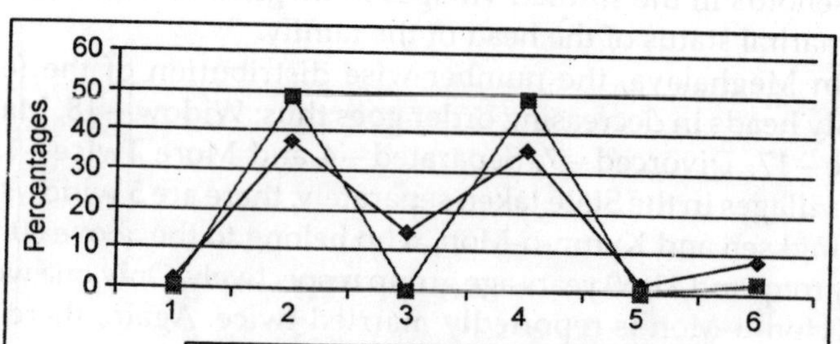

1—Unmarried, 2—Widow, 3—Divorced, 4—Married Once, 5—Married more than once, 6—Separated

Fig. 7.23: Distribution of Female Headed Households by Marital Status in Meghalaya and Tripura

Table 7.13: Distribution of the Household Heads by their Preference for Children by Sex

State	Village	Sex	Literacy Status	Preference for Children by Sex				Subtotal	Total
				Like more male children	Like more female children	Male and female equal	Cannot say		
Meghalaya	Ringkseh	Male	Illiterate	0	0	0	1	25	45
			<Madhyamik	2	0	7	6		
			>Madhyamik	0	0	9	0		
		Female	Illiterate	0	0	1	1	20	
			<Madhyamik	4	8	1	2		
			>Madhyamik	0	1	2	0		
	Kyton-u-Mon	Male	Illiterate	0	0	4	2	22	50
			<Madhyamik	0	1	5	5		
			>Madhyamik	0	0	5	0		
		Female	Illiterate	2	2	4	8	28	
			<Madhyamik	0	0	5	3		
			>Madhyamik	1	0	2	1		
	Total	Male	Illiterate	0	0	4	3	47	95
			<Madhyamik	2	1	12	11		
			>Madhyamik	0	0	14	0		
		Female	Illiterate	2	2	5	9	48	
			<Madhyamik	4	8	6	5		
			>Madhyamik	1	1	4	1		
Tripura	Beltali	Male	Illiterate	0	1	2	2	36	55
			<Madhyamik	1	2	22	3		
			>Madhyamik	0	1	2	0		
		Female	Illiterate	2	0	10	1	19	
			<Madhyamik	0	1	5	0		
			>Madhyamik	0	0	0	0		

(Contd).

Table 7.13: *(Contd.)*

State Village	Sex	Literacy Status	Preference for Children by Sex				Sub Total	Total
			Like more male children	Like more female children	Male and female equal	Cannot say		
Kalitila	Male	Illiterate	0	0	4	1	36	54
		<Madhyamik	3	3	14	2		
		>Madhyamik	0	0	8	1		
	Female	Illiterate	3	0	5	1	18	
		<Madhyamik	0	1	8	0		
		>Madhyamik	0	0	0	0		
Total	Male	Illiterate	0	1	6	3	72	109
		<Madhyamik	4	5	36	5		
		>Madhyamik	0	1	10	1		
	Female	Illiterate	5	0	15	2	37	
		<Madhyamik	0	2	13	0		
		>Madhyamik	0	0	0	0		
Grand Total	Male	Illiterate	0	1	10	6	119	204
		<Madhyamik	6	6	48	16		
		>Madhyamik	0	1	24	1		
	Female	Illiterate	7	2	20	11	85	
		<Madhyamik	4	10	19	5		
		>Madhyamik	1	1	4	1		

relevant data on this aspect from the studied villages in the background of the literary status of the family heads and our findings have been represented in the table reproduced hereafter.

Table 7.13 gives us a clue about the village-wise distribution of the household heads in the two States of Meghalaya and Tripura by their preference for children by sex.

It is seen that in Ringkseh, Meghalaya, 16 male heads had no particular preference for children by sex and treated the male and female children in the family alike. The literacy status of 7 of these male heads was below Madhyamik and 9 of them above Madhyamik. Among the female heads in the village, however, the trend was quite different as only 4 of them disclosed that they treated the male children and female children alike. While as many as 9 female heads revealed their preference for female children, 4 of them admitted in the contrary that they preferred male children over female children. 7 male heads and 3 female heads in Ringkseh declined to disclose their preference. 75 per cent of the female heads in Ringkseh were educated below Madhyamik level.

Table 7.13 reveals that in Kyton-u-Mon, 27.27 per cent, 50 per cent and 22.7 per cent of the male heads were illiterate, below Madhyamik and above Madhyamik respectively. However, irrespective of their literacy status, as many as 14 male heads opined that they did not discriminate against their children in terms of sex. While none of the male heads here preferred male children over female, 1 of them expressed his preference for female children and said he would not mind if there were more female children in his family.

Among the females in Kyton-u-Mon, 11 revealed that they had no particular preference about the sex of their children and said they did not make any distinction between the female and the male children in the family. While 7 of these 11 female household heads in particular were literate, 4 were illiterate. Again, 12 female heads in the village were not ready to disclose their preferences. In totality, 16 out of 28 female heads in the village were illiterate, 8 were educated below Madhyamik level and 4 above Madhyamik level.

Thus it is clear that in Meghalaya, a total of 45 households out of the 95 households did not make any discrimination between the male and female children. As many as 29 household heads said they were unsure about their inclination and declined to disclose their preference of the children in the families by their sexes.

Shifting our attention to the two villages in Tripura next, we get to know that 13.88 per cent of the male heads and 59.45 per cent of the studied female heads in Beltali and Kalitila were illiterate.

In Beltali village, 26 out of the 36 male-headed households and 15 out of the 19 female-headed households did not make any distinction between the male and female children in the family and treated the children of both sexes alike. Again, as few as 1 male head and 2 female heads expressed their preference for male children while 4 male heads and 1 female head said they preferred female children to male children.

So far as Kalitila village is concerned, as many as 26 out of 36 male heads and 13 out of 18 female heads said they had no preference and treated all children alike. 4 male heads and 1 female head in the village declined from making any comments on their preference of male and female children.

Therefore it is clear that the villages in Tripura taken together, 52 out of 72 male heads and 28 out 37 female heads did not make any distinction between the male and female children in the households. It also gets revealed that while a majority of this category of male heads was literate, there was a greater number of illiterates among the females who did not discriminate against their children by their sex. This is a good sign indeed. However, there were 5 illiterate female heads who disclosed their preference for male children (Fig. 7.24).

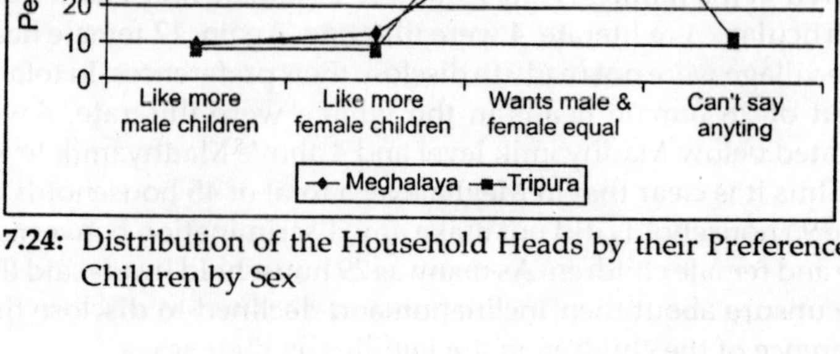

Fig. 7.24: Distribution of the Household Heads by their Preference for Children by Sex

(B) ECONOMIC EMPOWERMENT

Like in most civilized societies elsewhere, in India too, society has for long been a basically male-dominated one with the men alone enjoying economic empowerment. However, with the changing social structure and the improvement in people's life style, there has been a growing economic pressure, and it has to be admitted that the involvement of women in economic activities is no less important anymore. So, as in the rest of the world, in India too, things are changing and today a large number of women from all socio-economic groups are coming out of their homes to claim economic empowerment and earn a livelihood. The government of India and the State governments have been in the fore in respect of passing relevant Acts and policies for ensuring the economic empowerment of women.

The findings of our study in this context will be discussed in the pages that follow. Tables and Charts have been attached to verify the authenticity of the data collected.

Earning Status

What is the earning status of the male and female household heads of Ringkseh and Kyton-u-Mon villages in Meghalaya and Beltali and Kalitila villages in Tripura? Have the women in the two States benefited in any way by the economic empowerment granted to the women in India by the government? What is the distribution of the male heads by their earning status in a State like Meghalaya where the society is largely matrilineal? The study team has made relevant queries on the earning status of the household heads, which find representation in Table 7.14. Figs. 7.25 to 7.32 will substantiate the reliability of the next part of this discussion.

Meghalaya, as we all know, has a matrilineal family system. In addition, like in most hilly States, here too the women are basically more active than the males who, besides working less, consume a lot of liquor regularly. In other words, many of the males in the State are known to depend extensively on their female counterparts for providing them their basic needs. Of course, over the years, due to more males and females joining the literacy programmes, the attitude and thought-process of the State's people

Table 7.14: Distribution of Households by Earning Status of the Head of the Households

State	Village	Sex	Age Group	E/D		Sub Total	Total
				Dependent	Earner		
(1)	(2)	(3)	(4)	(5)	(6)	(7)	(8)
Meghalaya	Ringkseh	Male	20-40	1	7	25	45
			41-60	1	7	(55.56)	(47.37)
			>60	1	8		
		Female	20-40	1	3	20	
			41-60	0	8	(44.44)	
			>60	4	4		
	Kyton-u-Mon	Male	20-40	0	8	22	50
			41-60	0	10	(44)	(52.63)
			>60	0	4		
		Female	20-40	3	5	28	
			41-60	1	10	(56)	
			>60	0	9		
	Total	Male	20-40	1	15	47	95
			41-60	1	17	(49.47)	(46.57)
			>60	1	12		
		Female	20-40	4	8	48	
			41-60	1	18	(50.53)	
			>60	4	13		
Tripura	Beltali	Male	20-40	0	12	36	55
			41-60	1	15	(65.45)	(50.46)
			>60	3	5		
		Female	20-40	0	0	19	
			41-60	3	6	(34.55)	
			>60	9	1		

(Contd).

Table 7.14: (*Contd*).

State	*Village*	*Sex*	*Age Group*	*E/D*		*Sub Total*	*Total*
				Dependent	*Earner*		
(1)	*(2)*	*(3)*	*(4)*	*(5)*	*(6)*	*(7)*	*(8)*
	Kalitila	Male	20-40	2	16	36	54
			41-60	2	13	(66.67)	(49.54)
			>60	0	3		
		Female	20-40	2	1	18	
			41-60	3	4	(33.33)	
			>60	0	8		
	Total	Male	20-40	2	28	72	109
			41-60	3	28	(66.06)	(53.43)
			>60	3	8		
		Female	20-40	2	1	37	
			41-60	6	10	(33.94)	
			>60	9	9		
Grand Total		Male	20-40	3	43	119	204
			41-60	4	45	(58.33)	(100)
			>60	4	20		
		Female	20-40	6	9	85	
			41-60	7	28	(41.67)	
			>60	13	22		
		Total	20-40	9	52	204	
			41-60	11	73	(100)	
			>60	17	42		

have undergone sea-changes and the overall picture of the socio-economic situation changed a lot.

For instance, in Kyton-u-Mon village, not a single male household head is dependent on his female counterpart on economic grounds as all of them are engaged in some or the other activity and earn a livelihood. Rather among the female heads in the same village, there are 24 earners and 4 who are dependents on others and do not pursue any economic activity.

The situation is more or less the same in Ringkseh, where 22 out of the 25 male household heads are earners and the remaining 3 are dependents, implying that 93.62 per cent of the male heads in the village are earners. So far as the female heads of Ringkseh are concerned, there are 5 dependents and 15 earners in the 20 female-headed households. Both the villages taken together, 93.61 per cent of the male heads and 81.25 per cent of the female heads are earners. As such, only a small number of male heads and female heads could not, for some genuine reasons, make use of the economic opportunities that are available in the villages. Again, in Meghalaya, the ratio between the female earners and female dependents is 3 : 1 in Ringkseh and 6 : 1 in Kyton-u-Mon.

The situation in Tripura, on the other hand, is largely different. The society here follows a patriarchal family system and the females have evidently remained a subdued group for long. Under the patriarchal family system, the male members are automatically the breadwinners. As such a majority of the male heads (64 out of 72 male household heads) in the two villages of Tripura are earners.

However, as elsewhere in the country, with the changing life situation, the women in the State too are gaining economic independence and engaging themselves in economic activities, as available to them according to their literacy status, the growth pace varying from one place to another. As such, as revealed in Table 7.14, in Beltali village, 12 of the 19 female heads are dependent on others for a living, which makes it that 63.15 per cent of them are dependent and 36.85 per cent are earners. Contrastingly, in Kalitila, 13 of the 18 female heads, or 72.22 per cent of the female heads have ventured out of their homes out of economic compulsion and are contributing towards the family income. The ratio of the earning female heads and the dependent female heads is almost 1 : 1.7 in Beltali and 2.6 : 1 in Kalitila.

If we consider both the States as one unit, then it is found that

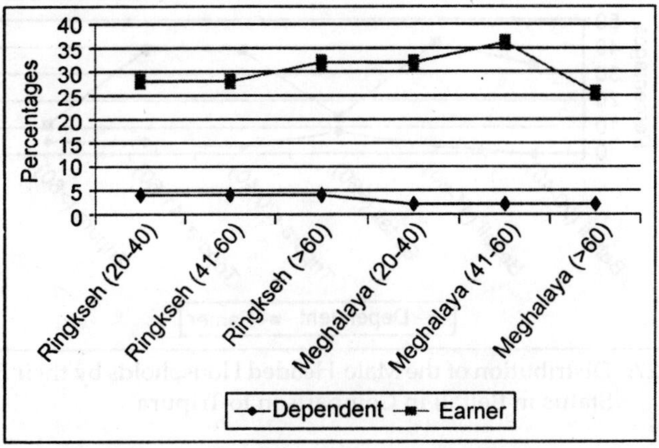

Fig. 7.25: Distribution of the Male-Headed Households by their Earning Status in Ringkseh in Comparison to Meghalaya

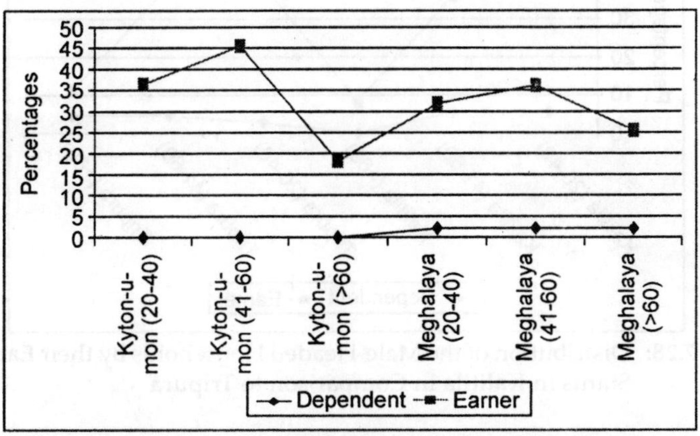

Fig. 7.26: Distribution of the Male-Headed Households by their Earning Status in Kyton-u-Mon in Comparison to Meghalaya

59 out of 85 female heads are earners and 26 are dependents. Again, while in Tripura the earner-dependent ratio of the female heads is almost 1 : 1 (total), in Meghalaya it is almost equal to 4.3 : 1 (Figs. 7.25 to 7.32).

Monthly Expenditure

Whether a male-headed household or a female-headed household,

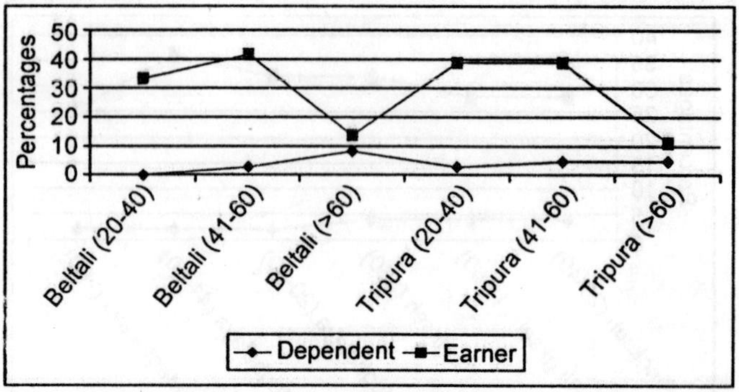

Fig. 7.27: Distribution of the Male-Headed Households by their Earning Status in Beltali in Comparison to Tripura

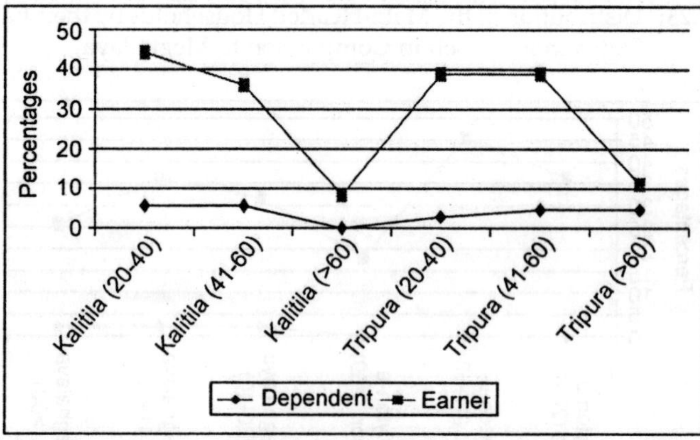

Fig. 7.28: Distribution of the Male-Headed Households by their Earning Status in Kalitila in Comparison to Tripura

every household in order to maintain itself, has to expend an amount of money, which may be fixed or variable, as per the changing family needs. However, every household tries to maintain a limit in its monthly expenditure. The households in the studied villages of Meghalaya and Tripura have also been interviewed in this regard in order to let us have an idea of the monthly expenditures of the families.

Table 7.15 lets the reader take a look at the monthly expenditure of the studied households in the four villages in Meghalaya and Tripura. The sample population has been grouped into five categories based on their monthly expenditure ranging—

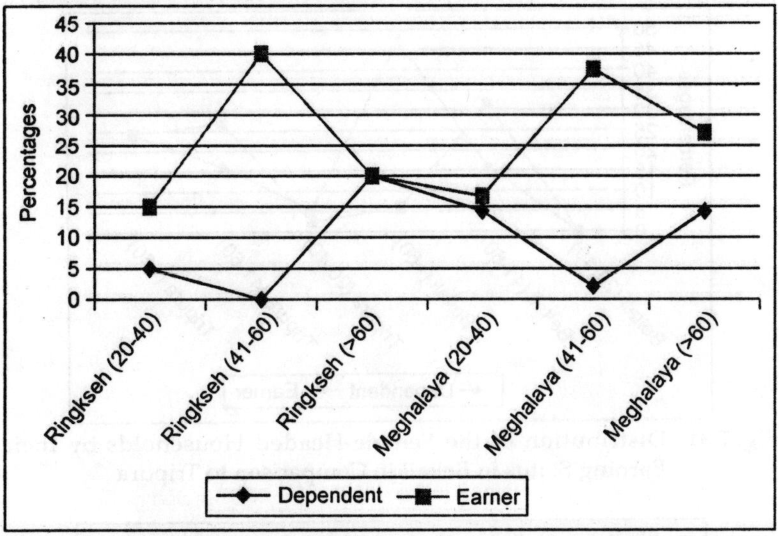

Fig. 7.29: Distribution of the Female-Headed Households by their Earning Status in Ringkseh in Comparison to Meghalaya

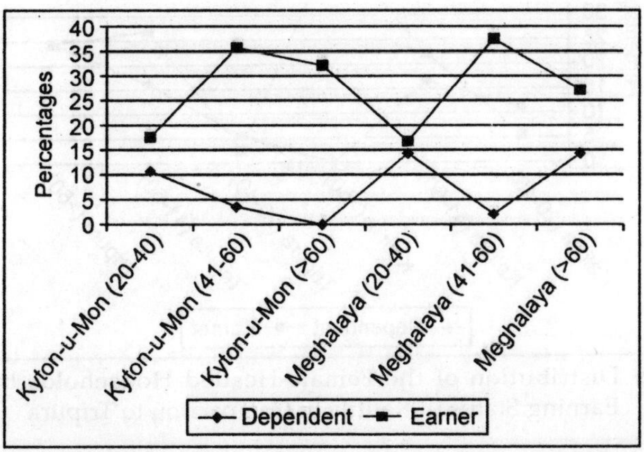

Fig. 7.30: Distribution of the Female-Headed Households by their Earning Status in Kyton-u-Mon in Comparison to Meghalaya

(i) below Rs. 1499,
(ii) between Rs. 1500–Rs. 2500,
(iii) between Rs. 2501–Rs. 4000,
(iv) between Rs. 4001–Rs. 5000, and
(v) above Rs. 5000.

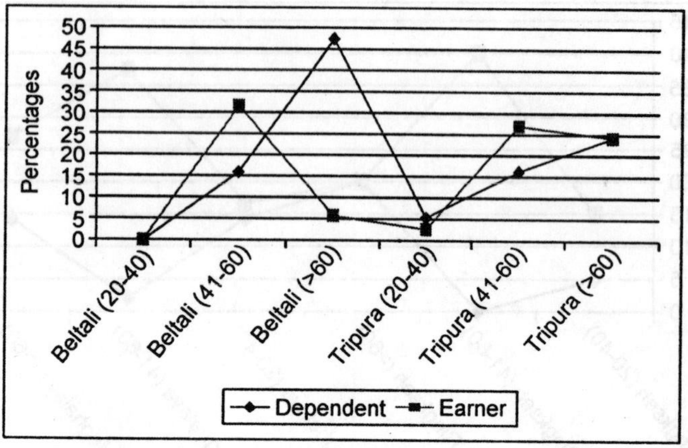

Fig. 7.31: Distribution of the Female-Headed Households by their Earning Status in Beltali in Comparison to Tripura

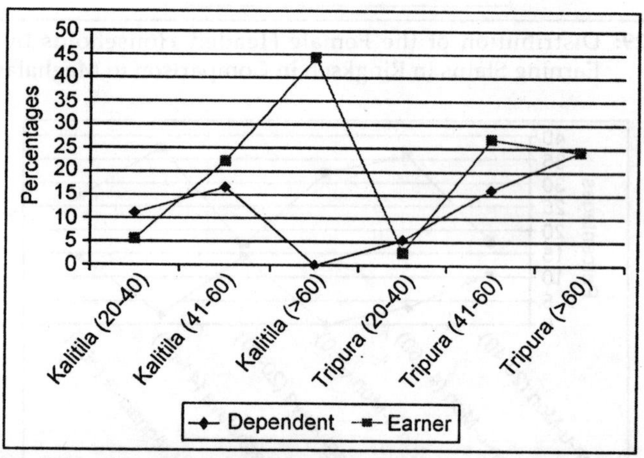

Fig. 7.32: Distribution of the Female-Headed Households by their Earning Status in Kalitila in Comparison to Tripura

From Table 7.15 it is evident that the households in the villages of Meghalaya belong to varied economic backgrounds, and hence, just as there are households that can not afford to spend even Rs. 1500 monthly, there are a few households with monthly expenditure running over Rs. 5000. We cannot comment on the standard of living of the families as that is decided not just by the monthly family expenditure, but also by the family size.

Table 7.15: Distribution of the Households by their Monthly Expenditure

State	Village	Sex	Monthly Expenditure					Sub Total	Total
			< 1499	1500-2500	2501- 4000	4001- 5000	> 5000		
(1)	(2)	(3)	(4)	(5)	(6)	(7)	(8)	(9)	(10)
Meghalaya	Ringkseh	Male	2 (8)	4 (16)	8 (32)	4 (16)	7 (28)	25 (55.56)	45 (47.37)
		Female	4 (20)	5 (25)	5 (25)	2 (10)	4 (20)	20 (44.44)	
	Kyton-u-Mon	Male	0	2 (9.09)	6 (27.27)	5 (22.73)	9 (40.91)	22 (44)	50 (52.63)
		Female	2 (7.14)	8 (28.57)	4 (14.29)	7 (25)	7 (25)	28 (56)	
	Total	Male	2 (4.26)	6 (12.77)	14 (29.79)	9 (19.15)	16 (34.04)	47 (49.47)	95 (46.57)
		Female	6 (12.5)	13 (27.08)	9 (18.75)	9 (18.75)	11 (22.92)	48 (50.53)	
Tripura	Beltali	Male	1 (2.78)	9 (25)	18 (50)	3 (8.33)	5 (13.89)	36 (65.45)	55 (50.46)
		Female	0	10 (52.63)	7 (36.84)	2 (10.53)	0	19 (34.55)	
	Kalitila	Male	1 (2.78)	10 (27.78)	16 (44.44)	4 (11.11)	5 (13.89)	36 (66.67)	54 (49.54)
		Female	4 (22.22)	2 (11.11)	8 (44.44)	1 (5.56)	3 (16.67)	18 (33.33)	
	Total	Male	2 (2.78)	19 (26.39)	34 (47.22)	7 (9.72)	10 (13.89)	72 (66.06)	109 (53.43)
		Female	4 (10.81)	12 (32.43)	15 (40.54)	3 (8.12)	3 (8.12)	37 (33.94)	
Grand Total		Male	4 (3.36)	25 (21.01)	48 (40.34)	16 (13.45)	26 (21.85)	119 (58.33)	204 (100)
		Female	10 (11.76)	25 (29.41)	24 (28.24)	12 (14.12)	14 (16.47)	85 (41.67)	
		Total	14 (6.86)	50 (24.51)	72 (35.29)	28 (13.73)	40 (19.61)	204 (100)	

In Table 7.15 we see that almost one-third of the total male heads in Ringktesh and Kyton-u-Mon reported that their monthly expenses go beyond Rs. 5000. These 16 male heads accounted for 34.04 per cent of the total male household heads in the two villages taken together. However, considered separately, while a maximum number of 9 male heads in Kyton-u-Mon belong to the 'Above Rs. 5000' monthly expenditure category, a maximum of 8 male heads in Ringkteh have said that their monthly expenses run between Rs. 2501 and Rs. 4000. It is also found from Table 7.15 for 'Distribution of the households by their monthly expenditure' that not a single male household head in Kyton-u-Mon village of Meghalaya has a monthly expenditure of less than Rs. 1499.

So far as the female heads in Meghalaya in the 'Above Rs. 5000' category are concerned, only 11 out of 48 female heads in the two named villages, which accounts for only 23 per cent of all the female heads, reported a monthly expenditure running above Rs. 5000. A majority of the female heads, on the other hand, said that their expenditure fluctuated in the Rs. 1500-Rs. 2500 category. For a considerable number of the female heads (18.75% each in the two specified categories), however, the monthly household expenditure is either in the Rs. 2501-Rs. 4000 or in the Rs. 4001-Rs. 5000 range. It is nevertheless very unfortunate that at least 12.77 per cent of the female heads in the two villages have a money power of less than Rs. 1499 for expending towards monthly expenditure.

A look at the situation in Tripura in respect of monthly household expenditure makes it evident that the money power of the surveyed villagers in the State is less than the spending power of the people of Meghalaya. That is because while only 10 per cent of the male heads in Tripura reported their monthly expenditure goes beyond Rs. 5000, in Meghalaya the per cent distribution in this category was in the tune of 34.04 per cent. Among the female heads too, in Tripura there are only 3 individuals only, accounting for 8.12 per cent of the total female heads, who could be grouped in the 'Above Rs. 5000' category for monthly expenditure. Besides, while in Meghalaya, the maximum number of male heads belong to the 'Above Rs. 5000' monthly expenditure category, the distribution of the male heads in the two villages of Tripura is maximum in the Rs. 2501 to Rs. 4000 category, with as many as 34 of them belonging here.

The villages taken separately, we may take note that there is not a single female household head in Beltali village of Tripura who has a monthly expenditure of less than Rs. 1499. However, a maximum of 52.63 per cent of the female heads in Beltali are concentrated in the Rs. 1500-Rs. 2500 monthly expenditure category.

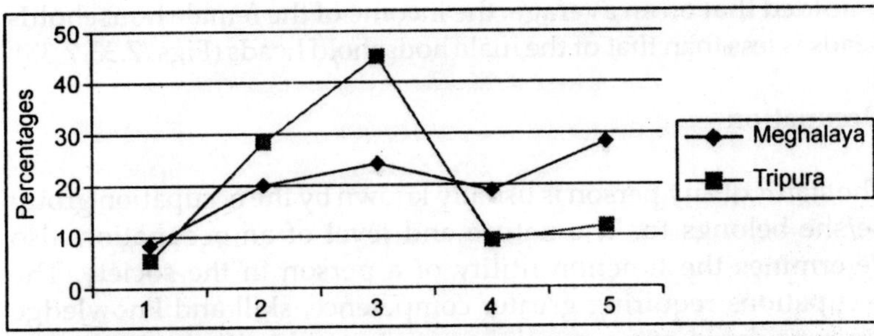

Fig. 7.33: Comparison of the Monthly Expenditures of the Total Household Heads (Male+Female) in Meghalaya and Tripura

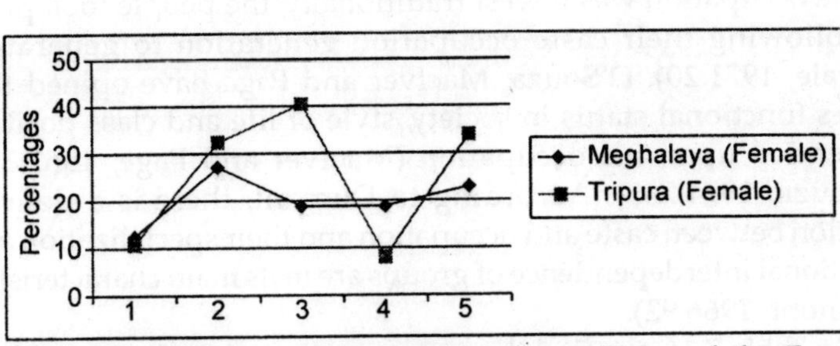

Fig. 7.34: Comparison of the Monthly Expenditure of the Female-Headed Households in Meghalaya and Tripura

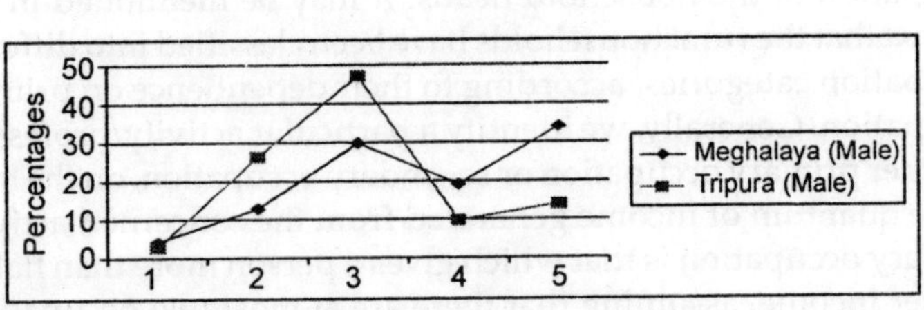

1→ Monthly expenditure less than 1499, 2 → Monthly expenditure 1500 to 2500, 3 → Monthly expenditure 2501 to 4000, 4 → Monthly expenditure 4001 to 5000, 5 Monthly expenditure more than 5000

Fig. 7.35: Comparison of the Monthly Expenditure of the Male-headed Households in Meghalaya and Tripura

It is also observed that 50 per cent of the male heads in Beltali and 44.44 per cent of the male heads in Kalitala are concentrated in the Rs. 2501 - Rs. 4000 monthly expenditure category.

From the grand total we may conclude that a maximum number of households are distributed in the category of 'Monthly Expenditure of Rs. 2501 - 4000'. Near about 35 per cent of the total households in both the States belong to this group. Again, it gets unfolded that on an average, the income of the female households heads is less than that of the male household heads (Figs. 7.33-7.35).

Occupation

The status of any person is usually known by the occupation group he/she belongs to. The nature and level of an occupation also determines the function utility of a person in the society. The occupations requiring greater competence, skill and knowledge are considered more prestigious and are identified with higher privileges and utilities. Borale points out that even when the status of the occupation was lowest traditionally, the people took pride in following their caste occupation generation to generation (Borale, 1971:20). D'Souza, MacIver and Page have opined that man's functional status in society, style of life and class position depended upon his occupation (MacIver and Page, 1962:390; D'Souza, 1974:265). According to Dumont, there is a definite relation between caste and occupation and their specialization and functional interdependence of groups are in its main characteristics (Dumont, 1966:92).

In Table 7.16, we find the representation of the households in the sample villages in Meghalaya and Tripura on the basis of the occupation of the household heads. It may be mentioned in this context that the rural households have been classified into different occupation categories, according to their dependence on primary occupation. Generally, we identify a particular activity/profession as either primary occupation or secondary occupation, on the basis of the quantum of income generated from the concerned activity. Primary occupation is that which gives a person more than half of his/her income, assuming that there are at most two occupations for a person.

It is expected that people having more than one occupation have greater access to the community. However, it has emerged

Table 7.16: Distribution of the Households by the Occupation of the Household Heads

State	Village	Sex	Literacy Status	Cultivator	Agriculture labourer + Unspecified Daily Labour	Govt. service	Private service	Business	House Wife	Old age	Others	Subtotal	Total
(1)	(2)	(3)	(4)	(5)	(6)	(7)	(8)	(9)	(10)	(11)	(12)	(13)	(14)
Meghalaya	Ringkseh	Male	Illiterate	0	0	0	0	0	0	1	0		
			<Madhyamik	2	8	1	0	3	0	0	1	25 (55.56)	
			>Madhyamik	0	3	4	1	0	0	0	1		
		Female	Illiterate	0	2	0	0	0	0	0	0		45 (47.37)
			<Madhyamik	0	3	0	0	4	1	4	3	20 (44.44)	
			>Madhyamik	0	0	2	0	1	0	0	0		
	Kyton-u-Mon	Male	Illiterate	0	4	0	2	0	0	0	0		
			<Madhyamik	2	5	0	3	1	0	0	0	22 (44)	
			>Madhyamik	0	0	3	0	2	0	0	0		
		Female	Illiterate	1	5	0	0	2	2	4	2		50 (52.63)
			<Madhyamik	1	2	0	1	2	1	0	1	28 (56)	
			>Madhyamik	0	0	1	1	1	0	0	1		

(Contd.)

Table 7.16 — *Contd.*

(1)	(2)	(3)	(4)	(5)	(6)	(7)	(8)	(9)	(10)	(11)	(12)	(13)	(14)
Meghalaya	Total	Male	Illiterate	0	4	0	2	0	0	1	0	47 (49.47)	95 (46.57)
			<Madhyamik	4	13	1	3	4	0	0	1		
			>Madhyamik	0	3	7	1	2	0	0	1		
		Female	Illiterate	1	7	0	0	2	2	4	2	48 (50.53)	
			<Madhyamik	1	5	0	1	6	2	4	4		
			>Madhyamik	0	0	3	1	2	0	0	1		
Tripura	Beltali	Male	Illiterate	1	2	0	0	0	0	0	2	36 (65.45)	55 (50.46)
			<Madhyamik	4	11	8	0	1	0	0	4		
			>Madhyamik	0	0	2	0	0	0	0	1		
		Female	Illiterate	0	2	0	0	0	9	0	2	19 (34.55)	
			<Madhyamik	0	0	0	0	0	6	0	0		
			>Madhyamik	0	0	0	0	0	0	0	0		
	Kalitila	Male	Illiterate	0	2	0	1	0	0	1	1	36 (66.67)	54 (49.54)
			<Madhyamik	2	10	3	3	1	0	0	3		
			>Madhyamik	2	1	0	1	1	0	0	4		
		Female	Illiterate	0	0	0	0	0	7	0	2	18 (33.33)	
			<Madhyamik	0	0	3	0	0	4	0	2		
			>Madhyamik	0	0	0	0	0	0	0	0		

(Contd.)

Table 7.16 — *Contd.*

(1)	(2)	(3)	(4)	(5)	(6)	(7)	(8)	(9)	(10)	(11)	(12)	(13)	(14)
Tripura	Total	Male	Illiterate	1	4	0	1	0	0	1	3	72 (66.06)	109 (53.43)
			<Madhyamik	6	21	11	3	2	0	0	7		
			>Madhyamik	2	1	2	1	1	0	0	5		
		Female	Illiterate	0	2	0	0	0	16	0	4	37 (33.94)	
			<Madhyamik	0	0	3	0	0	10	0	2		
			>Madhyamik	0	0	0	0	0	0	0	0		
Grand Total			Male	13 (10.9)	46 (38.66)	21 (17.65)	11 (9.24)	9 (7.56)	0	5 (4.20)	10 (8.40)	119 (58.33)	204 (100)
			Female	2 (2.35)	14 (16.47)	6 (7.06)	2 (2.35)	10 (11.76)	30 (35.29)	10 (11.76)	15 (17.65)	85 (41.67)	
			Total	15 (7.35)	60 (29.41)	27 (13.26)	13 (6.37)	19 (9.31)	30 (14.71)	15 (7.35)	25 (12.25)	204 (100)	

that because of their being into more than one occupation, they usually find less time to devote to their families than their counterparts who pursue only one occupation.

The clear picture that emerges from Table 7.16, which shows the occupation patterns of the studied household heads in the villages of Meghalaya and Tripura, reveals that a maximum number of persons of these two States are unspecified daily labourers.

A maximum of the agricultural labourers in Meghalaya, both males and females, are illiterate. On the other hand, only 4 male heads and 2 female heads, who are agricultural labours, in the two villages of Beltali and Kalitila of Tripura, are illiterate.

Moreover, most of the others in the 'Agricultural Labour' category in Tripura, are literate below Madhyamik level, while a few of them pursued their studies beyond the Madhyamik level too. It gets unfolded that no literate females in Tripura are engaged as agricultural labours in either of the villages in Tripura. Contrastingly, at least 21 male agricultural labours from the same two villages are educated below Madhyamik.

So far as the urgency to fill up government posts in the two States is concerned, we found that there are only 8 males and 3 females out of a total 45 household heads in Ringkseh and Kyton-u-Mon (Meghalaya), who are engaged in government service for a livelihood and 13 males and just 3 females among the 95 household heads in Beltali and Kalitila (Tripura), who earn a livelihood by pursuing government service. This means that only 24.4 per cent of the total household heads in Ringkseh and Kyton-u-Mon and 16.84 per cent of the total households in Tripura who have opted to fill up government posts. None of the respondents who are engaged in government services are illiterate.

Another interesting fact that is contrasting about the occupation patterns of the female heads in the two States is that while in Meghalaya, where the matrilineal system is in vogue, there is a very small group of women who are housewives—only 4 out of the total 48 females heads (8.33%), in Tripura, a maximum number of women—26 out of the total 37 female heads (70.27%)—belong to the 'housewife' category. On the other hand, while in Meghalaya a considerable number of female household heads (almost 21%) pursue business as an occupation, in Tripura, the

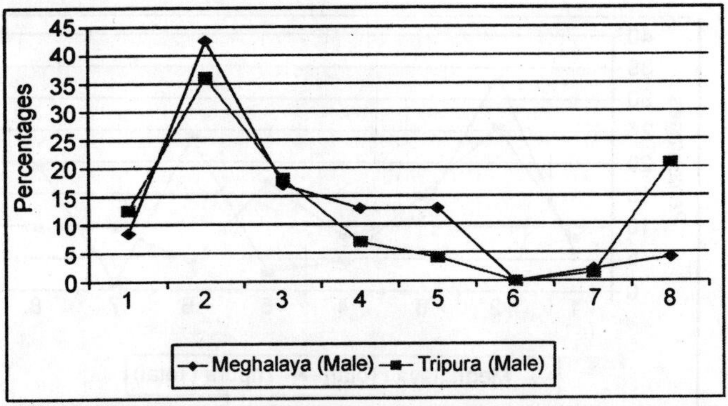

Fig. 7.36: Comparison of the Occupation of the Male Household Heads in Meghalaya and Tripura

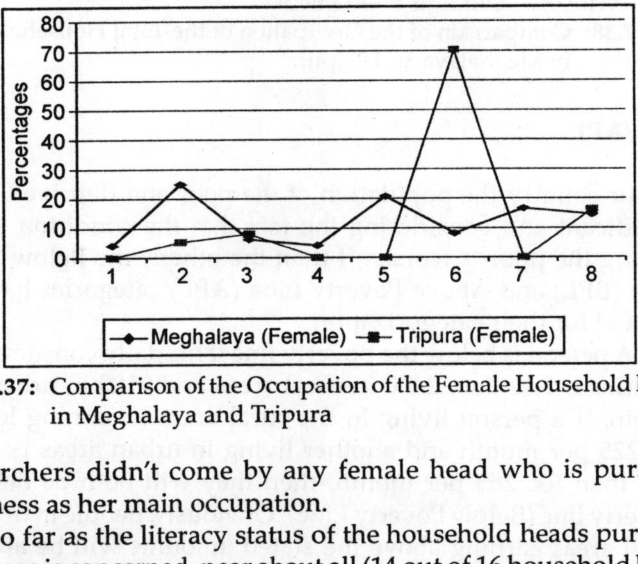

Fig. 7.37: Comparison of the Occupation of the Female Household Heads in Meghalaya and Tripura

researchers didn't come by any female head who is pursuing business as her main occupation.

So far as the literacy status of the household heads pursuing business is concerned, near about all (14 out of 16 household heads engaged in business) are educated.

Similarly, out of the 60 household heads from both the States who are engaged as agricultural labourers, irrespective of sex, 17 household heads are 'illiterate' while 42 belong to the 'less than Madhyamik' group and only 1 belongs to the 'more than Madhyamik' group (Figs. 7.36 – 7.38).

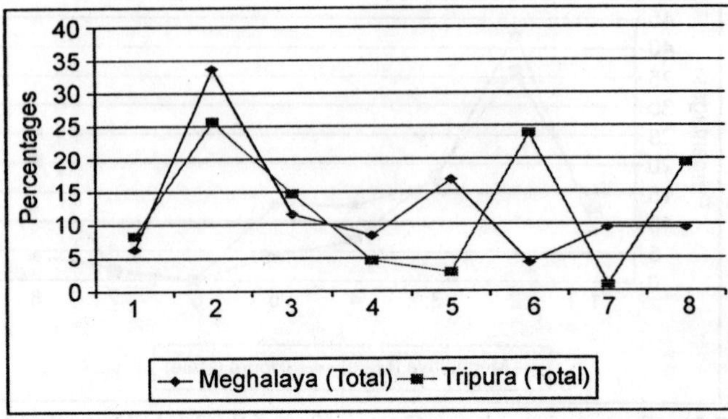

Note: 1 — Cultivator, 2 — Agriculture Labour + Unspecified Daily Labour, 3 — Govt. Service, 4 — Private Service, 5 — Business, 6 — House Wife, 7 — Old Age, 8 — Others.

Fig. 7.38: Comparison of the Occupation of the Total Household Heads in Meghalaya and Tripura

BPL/APL

In our country the population of the poor and deprived is quite significant and considering the fact that the condition of some among the poor is worse off than the others, the Below Poverty Line (BPL) and Above Poverty Line (APL) categories have been created for their categorization.

A person is below the poverty line if his daily consumption of calories is less than 2400 in rural areas and 2100 in urban areas. Again, if a person living in the rural areas is earning less than Rs. 225 per month and another living in urban areas is earning less than Rs. 265 per month, then they will both be below the poverty line (Below Poverty Line). Obviously, people in urban and rural areas earning above the stated amounts will be above the poverty line (Above Poverty Line).

Table 7.17 shows the distribution of the household heads in the sample villages of Meghalaya and Tripura by their BPL/APL (*) status as against sex. Considering the current poverty line (per capita yearly income as Rs. 392) for India, it is seen that only 11.6 per cent households in Meghalaya and 13.8 per cent households in Tripura are below poverty line households.

Taken separately, 93.62 per cent of the male heads and 83.33 per cent of the female heads in Ringkteh and Kyton-u-Mon belong

Table 7.17: Distribution of the Household Heads by BPL/APL (*) Status as against Sex

State	*Village*	*Sex*	*Family Type*		*Sub Total*	*Total*
(1)	(2)	(3)	(4)		(5)	(6)
			BPL	*APL*		
Meghalaya	Ringkseh	Male	2 (8)	23 (92)	25 (55.56)	45 (47.37)
		Female	3 (15)	17 (85)	20 (44.44)	
	Kyton-u-Mon	Male	1 (4.55)	21 (95.45)	22 (44)	50 (52.63)
		Female	5 (17.86)	23 (82.14)	28 (56)	
	Total	Male	3 (6.38)	44 (93.62)	47 (49.47)	95 (46.57)
		Female	8 (16.67)	40 (83.33)	48 (50.53)	
Tripura	Beltali	Male	5 (13.89)	31 (86.11)	36 (65.45)	55 (50.46)
		Female	3 (15.79)	16 (84.21)	19 (34.55)	
	Kalitila	Male	3 (8.33)	33 (91.67)	36 (66.67)	54 (49.54)
		Female	4 (22.22)	14 (77.78)	18 (33.33)	
	Total	Male	8 (11.11)	64 (88.89)	72 (66.06)	109 (53.43)
		Female	7 (18.92)	30 (81.08)	37 (33.94)	
Grand Total		Male	11 (9.24)	108 (90.76)	119 (58.33)	204 (100)
		Female	15 (17.65)	70 (82.35)	85 (41.67)	
		Total	26 (12.75)	178 (87.25)	204 (100)	

to the APL category. Similarly, in Beltali and Kalitila of Tripura also, 88.89 per cent of the males and 81.08 per cent of the females belong to the APL category. From this we could safely infer that although there are families that live below the poverty line, the

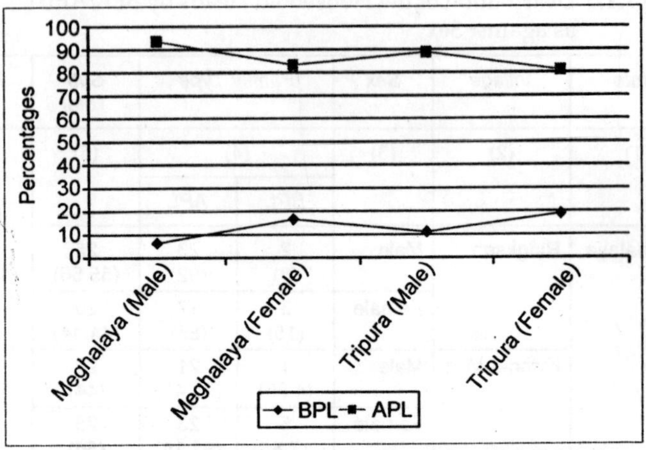

Fig. 7.39: Distribution of the Household Heads by BPL/APL Status

situation in the two north-eastern States, wherein the study has been conducted, is far better than the rest of India.

Interestingly, a comparison of the position of the male and female heads in the BPL category in Meghalaya reveals that the per cent of female household heads is more than double than that of the male household heads.

Property by Inheritance

Any kind of possessions in the form of land, building, car, wealth, jewelry, cash, etc., is considered as property. An individual makes property by own efforts or by inheritance. The research team that went to Meghalaya and Tripura for conducting this study, collected vital information about the assets and properties of the sample male and female heads. Table 7.18(a) reveals the distribution of the household heads by the property received by them by inheritance.

An important aspect that has to be remembered in the context of inheritance of property is that with Meghalaya having a matriarchal social set-up, it is expected that it is the women who would inherit the property left to them by their mothers. Contrarily, like in the rest of India, in Tripura too a patriarchal social system prevails, and hence, expectedly, it is the men who are likely to inherit their parental property. However, with the government

Table 7.18(a): Distribution of the Household Heads by any kind of Property received by Inheritance

State	Village	Sex	Received Property by inheritance			Sub Total	Total
			Received	Not Received	Others		
Meghalaya	Ringkseh	Male	11	14	0	25	45
		Female	11	9	0	20	
	Kyton-u-Mon	Male	10	12	0	22	50
		Female	10	18	0	28	
	Total	Male	21	26	0	47	95
		Female	21	27	0	48	
Tripura	Beltali	Male	21	13	2	36	55
		Female	4	14	1	19	
	Kalitila	Male	18	17	1	36	54
		Female	3	14	1	18	
	Total	Male	39	30	3	72	109
		Female	7	28	2	37	
Grand Total		Male	60	56	3	119	204
		Female	28	55	2	85	

having come out with a ruling that in patriarchal societies too, women would henceforth have a right to inherit a part of their parental property, the impact of the ruling may have caught up in the State too. Besides, was the matrilineal family set-up breaking away from its tradition?

As we see in Table 7.18(a), in Ringkseh village in Meghalaya, more number of females (11) have received property by inheritance in comparison to those who have not (9). In Kyton-u-Mon, on the other hand, there are more female (18) heads who did not receive any property by inheritance than those (10) who inherited parental property. The reason for this could be that among the Khasis, the inheritance edict delegates exclusive rights to the eldest daughter in the family to inherit the parental property. Of course, there have been some modifications by which provisions have been made to allow the other daughters in the family to inherit some share of the parental property, although the eldest daughter still has the right to the lion's share.

Coming next to Beltali in Tripura we see that a greater number of female heads (14 out of 19) have not inherited any property. While only 4 of the female heads in this village made some property

Table 7.18(b): Distribution of the Counterparts of the Household Heads by any kind of Property received by Inheritance

State	*Village*	*Sex*	*Received Property by inheritance*			*Sub Total*	*Total*
			Received	*Not Received*	*Others*		
Meghalaya	Ringkseh	Male	4	10	2	16	35
		Female	5	14	0	19	
	Kyton-u-Mon	Male	1	4	15	20	41
		Female	0	5	16	21	
	Total	Male	5	14	17	36	76
		Female	5	19	16	40	
Tripura	Beltali	Male	4	8	5	17	53
		Female	7	26	3	36	
	Kalitila	Male	4	10	0	14	50
		Female	3	31	2	36	
	Total	Male	8	18	5	31	103
		Female	10	57	5	72	
Grand Total		Male	13	32	22	67	179
		Female	15	51	21	87	

by inheritance, 1 female head made property through other resources. On the other hand, although a considerable number of the male heads in either Beltali (13) or Kalitila (17) of Tripura have not made any property by inheritance, a significant number of the males (39) inherited some parental property at least. 2 male heads from Beltali and 1 male head from Kalitila made property from other resources and did not have to depend on inheritance of parental property for ownership of property [Table 7.18(b)].

If we consider the counterparts of the household heads in Meghalaya for instance, then we shall see that only 13.15 per cent of the males and females together received property by inheritance. Similarly, only 17.45 per cent of the counterparts of the household heads in Tripura inherited part or whole of their parental property.

Thus, both the States taken together and the males and females considered as separate wholes, 19.40 per cent of all the male counterparts of the household heads and 17.24 per cent of all the female counterparts of the household heads have received property through inheritance (Fig. 7.40).

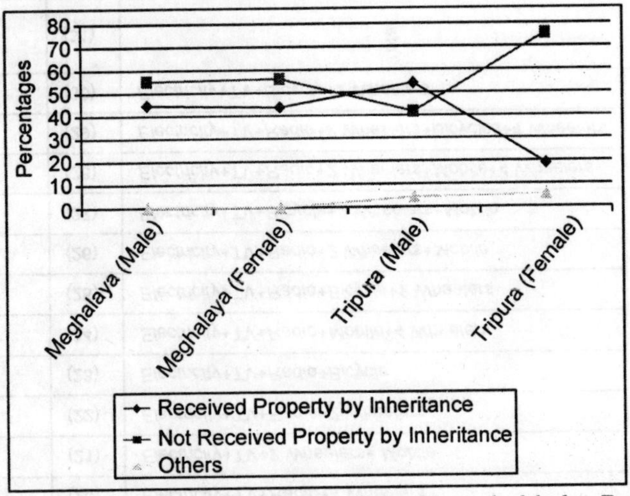

Fig. 7.40: Distribution of the Head of the Households by Received Property by Inheritance

Facilities and Assets

Today, thanks to man's inventive mind, the market is flooded with facilities and assets in the form of goods and gadgets that make life easier and comfortable for him. However, it is an individual's personal economic strength that allows him to avail of all or many of these gadgets; hence the ownership of the gadgets indirectly reflects a person's economic status and capacity too. The common facilities and assets that have been taken into consideration during data collection on assets and facilities are—electricity, TV, radio, bicycles, mobiles two wheelers and four wheelers.

From Table 7.19 it gets revealed that as many as 14 (out of 45) households in Ringkseh, 22 (out of 50) households in Kyton-u-Mon, 12 (out of 55) in Beltali and 5 (out of 54) in Kalitila are provided with electricity exclusively.

Table 7.19 also shows that as many as 15 households in Meghalaya and 12 households in Tripura are not provided with any facilities and that only 2 households in Kalitila in Tripura are owners of only a bicycle; they have to do without electricity. In contrast, 2 households in Ringkseh and Kyton-u-Mon in Meghalaya are provided with assets like electricity, television, radio, two-wheeler, mobile and four-wheeler and 1 household in

Table 7.19: Distribution of the Households by their Facilities and Assets

State	Village	Assets and Facilities																												Total
		Electricity	TV	Radio	Bicycles	Nothing	Electricity+TV	Electricity + Bicycles	Electricity + Radio	Electricity+Mobile	Electricity+TV+Radio	Electricity+TV+4 Wheelers	Electricity+TV+Mobile	Electricity+TV+Bicycle	Electricity+Radio+Bicycle	Electricity+TV+2 Wheelers	TV+Bicycle+2 Wheelers	Electricity+TV+Radio+Mobile	Electricity+TV+Radio+4 Wheelers	Electricity+TV+2 Wheelers+ Mobile	Electricity+TV+Radio+2 Wheelers	Electricity+TV+Radio+Bicycle	Electricity+TV+Radio+Mobile+4 Wheelers	Electricity+TV+Radio+Bicycle+2 Wheelers	Electricity+TV+Radio+2 Wheelers+Mobile	Electricity+TV+Bicycle+2 Wheelers+Mobile	Electricity+TV+Radio+2 Wheelers+Mobile+4 Wheelers	Electricity+TV+Radio+2 Wheelers+Bicycles+4 Wheelers	Electricity+TV+Bicycle+2 Wheelers	
(1)	(2)	(3)	(4)	(5)	(6)	(7)	(8)	(9)	(10)	(11)	(12)	(13)	(14)	(15)	(16)	(17)	(18)	(19)	(20)	(21)	(22)	(23)	(24)	(25)	(26)	(27)	(28)	(29)	(30)	(31)
	Ringkseh	14	0	1	0	5	6	0	6	0	3	0	1	0	0	0	0	1	0	1	1	0	3	1	1	0	1	0	0	45

(Contd.)

Table 7.19 — *Contd.*

(1)	(2)	(3)	(4)	(5)	(6)	(7)	(8)	(9)	(10)	(11)	(12)	(13)	(14)	(15)	(16)	(17)	(18)	(19)	(20)	(21)	(22)	(23)	(24)	(25)	(26)	(27)	(28)	(29)	(30)	(31)
Meghalaya	Kyton-u-Mon	22	1	1	0	10	2	0	0	1	5	1	0	0	0	0	0	3	1	0	0	0	2	0	0	0	1	0	0	50
	Total	36	1	2	0	15	8	0	6	1	8	1	1	0	0	0	0	4	1	1	1	0	5	1	1	0	2	0	0	95
Tripura	Beltali	12	0	1	0	4	11	4	0	0	0	0	0	11	2	0	1	0	0	0	0	8	0	0	0	0	0	1	0	55
	Kalitila	5	1	0	2	8	10	3	1	0	0	1	0	14	0	2	0	0	0	1	1	2	0	1	0	1	0	0	1	54
	Total	17	1	1	2	12	21	7	1	0	0	1	0	25	2	2	1	0	0	1	1	10	0	1	0	1	0	1	1	109
Grand Total		53	2	3	2	27	29	7	7	1	8	2	1	25	2	1	1	4	1	2	2	10	5	2	1	1	2	1	1	204

Beltali in Tripura is provided with electricity, television, radio, bicycle, two-wheeler and four-wheeler, suggesting that these few households are economically well-off.

14 households in Meghalaya own either a television or a radio along with electricity facilities. 8 households in Meghalaya provided with electricity have both a television and a radio. There are 3 households in Meghalaya that are not provided with electricity although they possess either a radio or a television. 9 households in the State own four-wheelers. 6 households in Meghalaya are reported to have two-wheelers. At least 15 household heads in the State own a mobile phone.

In Tripura, while 17 households were provided with electricity as a lone facility. 21 households provided with electric connection own only a television set, while only 1 household provided with electricity facility owns a radio exclusively. Interestingly, although there is 1 household in Kalitila that has a radio and another household in Beltali that owns a television set, neither of the two households are provided with the facility of electricity. However, in Tripura, none of the households provided with electricity connection reported owning both a television set and a radio set at a time.

It may be noted that there are some 25 households in Beltali and Kalitila taken together that have electricity, TV and bicycle. However, none of the households in the two villages in Meghalaya possess the same facilities in this combination. Also, if we take a careful look at Table 7.19, we will notice that the possession of mobile phones, four wheelers and two wheelers in the villages of Tripura is less popular than in the villages of Meghalaya, implying that the affordability of the household heads from Meghalaya is higher than the heads in Tripura (Fig. 7.41).

(C) POLITICAL EMPOWERMENT

Inclusion in Voters' List and Exercising of Voting Power

An individual's residential status is strengthened, or rather, is officially recognised when his/her name figures in the Voters' List and when he/she is granted voting rights by the State. As per the laws of the land, any person, whether male or female, automatically becomes eligible to vote as soon as he/she becomes 18 years of

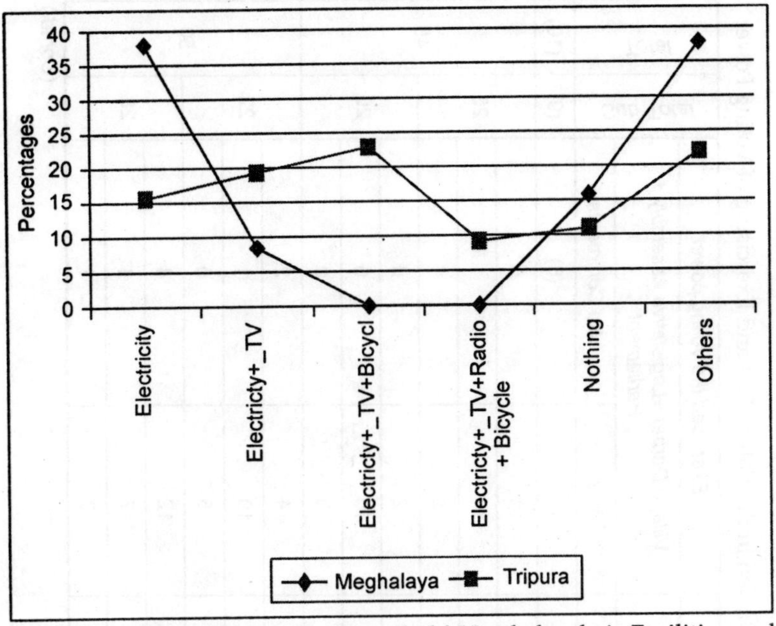

Fig. 7.41: Distribution of the Household Heads by their Facilities and Assets

age. The concerned person has to inform the local office of the Election Commission about having attained the age of 18 so that the process of enlisting his/her name in the Voters' List is accomplished promptly. An attempt has also been made by the study team to extract some relevant data from the household heads regarding the inclusion of their names in the Voters' List and other connected matters.

Table 7.20 shows that most of the interviewed household heads have been responsive to the researchers queries regarding the inclusion of their names in the official Voters' List. In the villages of Meghalaya, for instance, except 5 male heads and 6 female heads (comprising 11.57% of the total households), who refused to make any comments, all the others, the females included, have responded in the positive when asked if or not their names figure in the Voters' List. In Tripura, however, the non-responses came from 8 male heads and 1 female head, which together make up .08 per cent of the total households in Beltali and Kalitila covered by the study.

Table 7.20: Distribution of the Household Heads by their Inclusion in the Voters' List and Exercising of Voting Power

State	Village	Sex	Literacy Status	Inclusion in voting list: Village Darbar +Legislative Assembly +Parliament		Exercised the voting power: Village Darbar +Legislative Assembly + Parliament		Sub Total	Total
				Yes	No Comments	Yes	No Comments		
(1)	(2)	(3)	(4)	(5)	(6)	(7)	(8)	(9)	(10)
Meghalaya	Ringkseh	Male	Illiterate	1	0	1	0	25	45
			<Madhyamik	14	1	14	1		
			>Madhyamik	8	1	8	1		
		Female	Illiterate	2	0	2	0	20	
			<Madhyamik	15	0	15	0		
			>Madhyamik	3	0	3	0		
	Kyton-u-Mon	Male	Illiterate	4	2	4	2	22	50
			<Madhyamik	10	1	10	1		
			>Madhyamik	5	0	5	0		
		Female	Illiterate	12	4	12	4	28	
			<Madhyamik	7	1	7	1		
			>Madhyamik	3	1	3	1		

(Contd.)

Table 7.20: — *Contd.*

(1)	(2)	(3)	(4)	(5)	(6)	(7)	(8)	(9)	(10)
Meghalaya	*Total*	*Male*	Illiterate	5	2	5	2	47	95
			<Madhyamik	24	2	24	2		
			>Madhyamik	13	1	13	1		
		Female	Illiterate	14	4	14	4	48	
			<Madhyamik	22	1	22	1		
			>Madhyamik	6	1	6	1		
Tripura	*Beltali*	*Male*	Illiterate	2	3	2	3	36	55
			<Madhyamik	28	0	22	6		
			>Madhyamik	3	0	3	0		
		Female	Illiterate	13	0	13	0	19	
			<Madhyamik	6	0	5	1		
			>Madhyamik	0	0	0	0		
	Kalitila	*Male*	Illiterate	3	2	3	2	36	54
			<Madhyamik	20	2	19	3		
			>Madhyamik	8	1	7	2		
		Female	Illiterate	8	1	8	1	18	
			<Madhyamik	9	0	8	1		
			>Madhyamik	0	0	0	0		

(Contd.)

Table 7.20: — *Contd.*

(1)	(2)	(3)	(4)	(5)	(6)	(7)	(8)	(9)	(10)
Tripura	*Total*	*Male*	Illiterate	5	5	5	5	72	109
			<Madhyamik	48	2	41	9		
			>Madhyamik	11	1	10	2		
		Female	Illiterate	21	1	21	1	37	
			<Madhyamik	15	0	13	2		
			>Madhyamik	0	0	0	0		

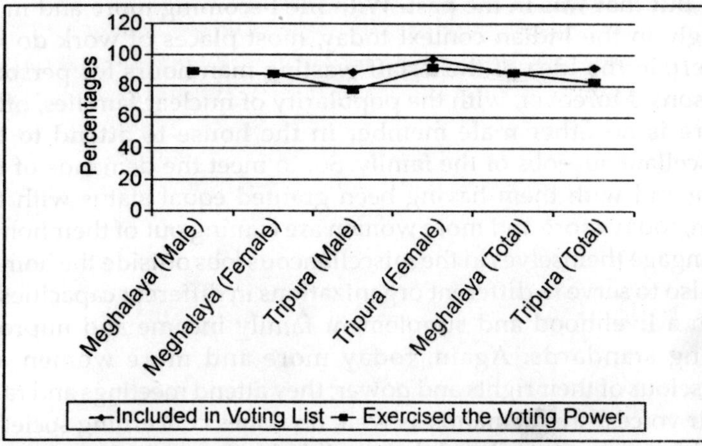

Fig. 7.42: Distribution of the Household Heads by their Inclusion in the Voters' List and Exercising of their Voting Power

All the household heads who responded in the positive when asked if or not their names figured in the Voters' List admitted without any hesitation about having participated in the election process by exercising their right to vote (Fig. 7.42).

Attendance in any Meeting

Even a few decades ago, our society was not as forward-looking as it is today and between men and women, the latter were expected to remain indoors and attend to all kinds of domestic chores the whole day. It were the men who had to make time from within their office hours and attend to many kinds of odd jobs like going to banks, post-offices, paying insurance dues or property tax, visiting markets and grocery shops, escorting their children to and from schools, so on and so forth. Similarly, when it came to politics, meetings and processions, etc., it were the men who attended them as was expected. It would be wrong to say that women's participation in meetings, etc., was totally absent for there was a handful of women, mostly belonging to the economically and culturally elite families, who used to participate in meetings, discussions and other related activities. The involvement of women from the conservative social sections as well as the ordinary classes in suchlike activities was very insignificant.

But that was in the past. With life becoming more and more tough, in the Indian context today, most places of work do not entertain the idea of their staff wasting man-hours for personal reasons. Moreover, with the popularity of nuclear families, often there is no other male member in the house to attend to the miscellaneous jobs of the family. So, to meet the demands of the time and with them having been granted equal status with the men, today more and more women are coming out of their homes to engage themselves in the miscellaneous jobs outside the homes, as also to serve in different organizations in different capacities to earn a livelihood and supplement family income and improve living standards. Again, today more and more women are conscious of their rights and power; they attend meetings and raise their voices, and demands as well, on issues concerning society's well-being in general and their well-being in particular.

But what is the level of participation of the sample people of the two States covered by our study? Table 7.21(a) will itself explain about the participation level of the different household heads in each of the sample villages in Meghalaya and Tripura in meetings and related activities.

Table 7.21(a): Distribution of the Counterparts of the Household Heads according to their Attendance in any kind of Meeting

State	*Village*	*Sex*	*Attend any meeting arranged by*			*Sub Total*	*Total*
			Panchayat	*Panchayat and Others*	*No Response*		
Meghalaya	Ringkseh	Male	21	0	4	25	45
		Female	19	0	1	20	
	Kyton-u-Mon	Male	17	4	1	22	50
		Female	21	6	1	28	
	Total	Male	38	4	5	47	95
		Female	40	6	2	48	
Tripura	Beltali	Male	6	22	8	36	55
		Female	7	5	7	19	
	Kalitila	Male	8	23	5	36	54
		Female	7	6	5	18	
	Total	Male	14	45	13	72	109
		Female	14	11	12	37	
Grand Total		Male	52	49	18	119	204
		Female	54	17	14	85	

From Table 7.21(a) it is evident that in either of the States, the level of participation of the people in meetings arranged by the Panchayat or Block Office is quite high. Almost 89.36 per cent of the male household heads and 95.83 per cent of the female household heads in Meghalaya confirmed their attendance in meetings of the Panchayat and others.

In Tripura, however, the male and female heads compare less than their counterparts in Meghalaya in this respect, with 81.94 per cent and 67 per cent of the male and female household heads respectively having attended suchlike meetings. Again, among the male and female heads in Tripura exclusively, the proportion of female heads who attend the meeting is significantly less, considering the fact that the people of the State are more politically conscious.

Table 7.21(b): Distribution of the Counterparts of the Household Heads according to their Attendance in any kind of Meeting

State	*Village*	*Sex*	*Attend any meeting arranged by*			*Sub Total*	*Total*
			Pancha-yat	*Pancha-yat and Others*	*No Response*		
Meghalaya	Ringkseh	Male	12	0	4	16	35
		Female	17	0	2	19	
	Kyton-u-Mon	Male	14	3	3	20	41
		Female	18	3	0	21	
	Total	Male	26	3	7	36	76
		Female	35	3	2	40	
Tripura	Beltali	Male	5	11	1	17	53
		Female	8	8	20	36	
	Kalitila	Male	3	11	0	14	50
		Female	10	6	20	36	
	Total	Male	8	22	1	31	103
		Female	18	14	40	72	
Grand Total		Male	34	25	8	67	179
		Female	53	17	42	112	

It is evident from Table 7.21(b) that overall, most of the counterparts of the household heads, whether male or female, have been actively participating in meetings and discussions organized from time to time by the Panchayat and other local level/national level political parties. It is, however, surprising that compared to Meghalaya, the female counterparts of the household heads in both the villages in Tripura, i.e., Beltali and Kalitila are less active in so far as their participation in meetings arranged by the Panchayat, etc., are concerned. In fact, only 44.44 per cent each of the female counterparts in the villages in Tripura reported having attended meetings arranged by the Panchayat and Block Office (Fig. 7.43).

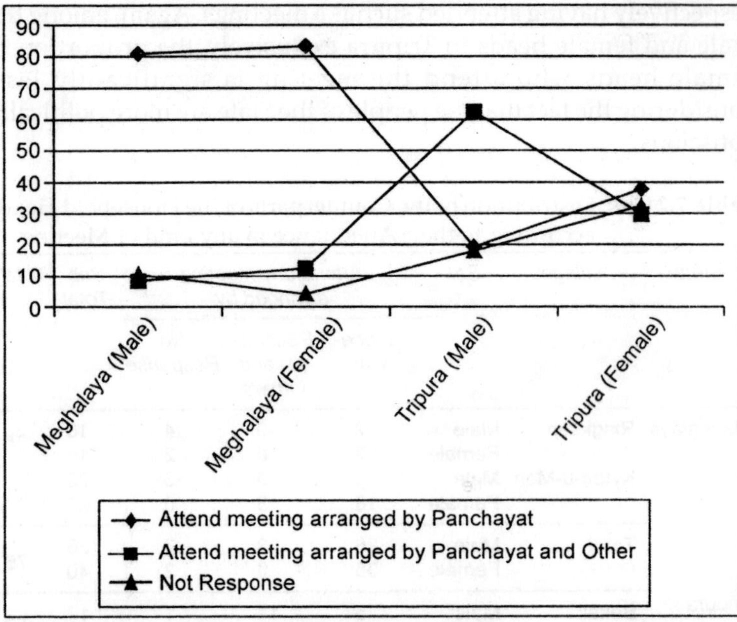

Fig. 7.43: Distribution of the Household Heads according to the Attendance in any kind of Meeting

(D) SOCIAL EMPOWERMENT

The social empowerment of an individual is reflected by his/her position in society, his/her raised consciousness about various social issues, his/her participation in social affairs, including his/her membership in clubs and suchlike bodies. While conducting the research study in the villages in Meghalaya and Tripura, the researchers have also collected relevant data pertaining to the household heads' membership in clubs, community centres or

Table 7.22(a): Distribution of the Household Heads by their Membership in Clubs/Community Centres/Social Organizations

State	*Village*	*Sex*	*Literacy Status*	*Member of Club/Community Centre/Social Organization*		*Sub Total*	*Total*
				Yes	*No*		
Meghalaya	Ringkseh	Male	Illiterate	0	1		
			< Madhyamik	5	10	25	
			> Madhyamik	5	4		
		Female	Illiterate	0	2		45
			< Madhyamik	1	14	20	
			> Madhyamik	0	3		
	Kyton-u-Mon	Male	Illiterate	0	6		
			< Madhyamik	1	10	22	
			> Madhyamik	1	4		
		Female	Illiterate	1	15		50
			< Madhyamik	0	8	28	
			> Madhyamik	0	4		
	Total	Male	Illiterate	0	7		
			< Madhyamik	6	20	47	
			> Madhyamik	6	8		
		Female	Illiterate	1	17		95
			< Madhyamik	1	22	48	
			> Madhyamik	0	7		
Tripura	Beltali	Male	Illiterate	0	5		
			< Madhyamik	7	21	36	
			> Madhyamik	1	2		
		Female	Illiterate	1	12		55
			< Madhyamik	0	6	19	
			> Madhyamik	0	0		
	Kalitila	Male	Illiterate	1	4		
			< Madhyamik	4	18	36	
			> Madhyamik	3	6		
		Female	Illiterate	8	1		54
			< Madhyamik	7	2	18	
			> Madhyamik	0	0		
	Total	Male	Illiterate	1	9		
			< Madhyamik	11	39	72	
			> Madhyamik	4	8		
		Female	Illiterate	9	13		109
			< Madhyamik	7	8	37	
			> Madhyamik	0	0		
Grand Total				46	158		204

social organizations in order to form an idea of his/her social empowerment.

Table 7.22(a) shows the distribution of the household heads in the sample villages in Meghalaya and Tripura by their membership in clubs/community centres/social oganizations. A fact that comes to the fore is that most of the household heads have not availed of membership in clubs and similar organizations. In fact, 83.33 per cent of the total households in the sample villages in these States are not members of any club, community centre or social organization.

If we review the distribution village-wise, we see that 60 per cent of the male heads and 95 per cent of the female heads in Ringkseh and 90.9 per cent and 96.42 per cent of the male and female heads in Kyton-u-Mon, both in Meghalaya did not take up any club membership and have not joined any community centre or social organization.

Turning our attention to the data on Tripura in the same Table, we see that 77.78 per cent and 94.73 per cent of the male and female heads respectively of Beltali and 77.78 per cent and 16.67 per cent of the female heads respectively of Kalitila responded in the negative when they were asked to confirm if or not they were members of any club or social organization. So, there is indeed a break in the trend in Kalitila among the female heads as unlike in the other villages, here approximately 83.33 per cent of them are actually members of any club, community centres or social organizations. In fact, if we see closely then we can see that the women of Kalitila, as compared to the men here, are more involved in the activities of the clubs and other social organizations.

Table 7.22(b) brings out the fact that most of the counterparts of the household heads (56.71% males and 89.28% females) in the two north-eastern States under review, did not possess any club membership. Neither did they get associated with any community centre or social organization (Fig. 7.44).

Membership in a Club/Community Centre/Social Organization/ NGO

In course of the survey and the interviews with the household heads and others in Meghalaya as well as Tripura it emerged that both the male heads and the female heads were still not particularly

Table 7.22(b): Distribution of the Counterparts of the Household Heads by their Membership in Clubs/Community Centres/Social Organizations

State	Village	Sex	Member of Club/Community Centre/Social Organization			Sub Total	Total
			Yes	No	Not answered		
Meghalaya	Ringkseh	Male	5	7	4	16	35
		Female	5	14	0	19	
	Kyton-u-Mon	Male	1	18	1	20	41
		Female	0	21	0	21	
	Total	Male	6	25	5	36	76
		Female	5	35	0	40	
Tripura	Beltali	Male	8	8	1	17	53
		Female	1	34	1	36	
	Kalitila	Male	7	5	2	14	50
		Female	4	31	1	36	
	Total	Male	15	13	3	31	103
		Female	5	65	2	72	
Grand Total		Male	21	38	8	67	179
		Female	10	100	2	112	

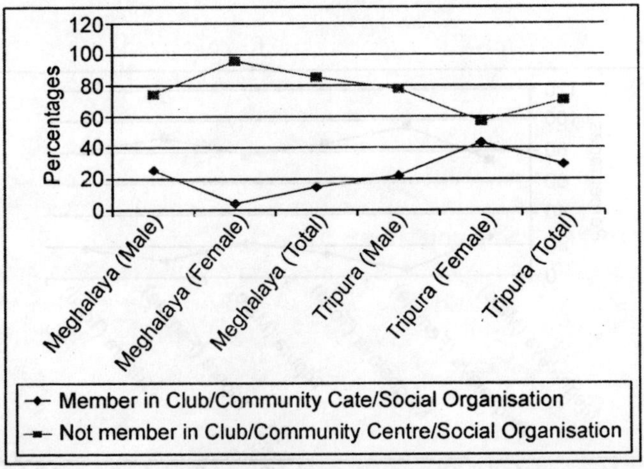

Fig. 7.44: Distribution of the Household Heads by their Membership in Clubs/Community Centres/Social Organizations

Table 7.23: Distribution of the Household Heads by their Membership in Clubs/Community Centres/Social Organizations/NGOs

State	*Village*	*Sex*	*Member of club/ community centre/social organization/NGO*		*Sub Total*	*Total*
			Yes	*No*		
Meghalaya	Ringkseh	Male	10	15	25	45
		Female	1	19	20	
	Kyton-u-Mon	Male	2	20	22	50
		Female	1	27	28	
	Total	Male	12	35	47	95
		Female	2	46	48	
Tripura	Beltali	Male	8	28	36	55
		Female	1	18	19	
	Kalitila	Male	8	28	36	54
		Female	3	15	18	
	Total	Male	16	56	72	109
		Female	4	33	37	
Grand Total		Male	28	91	119	204
		Female	6	79	85	

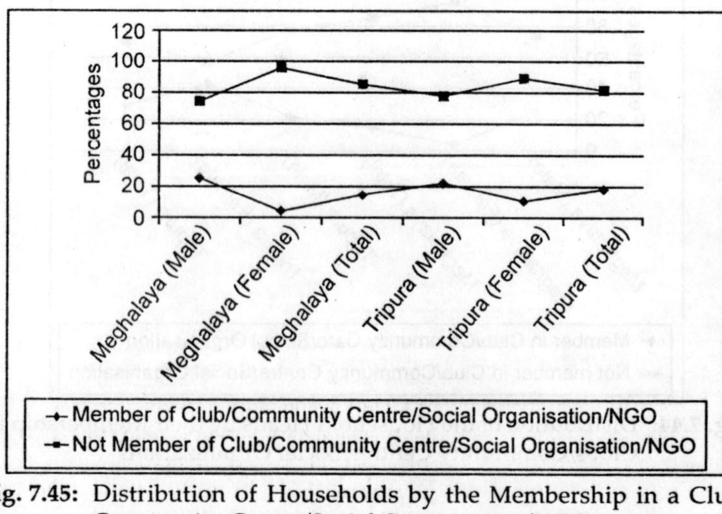

Fig. 7.45: Distribution of Households by the Membership in a Club/ Community Centre/Social Organization/NGO

inclined to get any club membership or join any community centre, social organization or NGO. From Table 7.23 it is clear that out of all the female-headed households taken together, there are very few female household heads (6 out of 85 female heads) who are members of any club or community centre or social organization or NGO. Similar is the case among the male heads also and a majority of them revealed that they were not members of any clubs, community centres, social organizations and NGOs. However, between the males and the females, the percentage of the male-heads (23.52%) who have joined any club etc., is higher than that of the female heads [(0.07%) see Fig. 7.45).

Table 7.24: Distribution of the Female-Headed Household Heads according to Participation in a Meeting/Function Outside the Village

State	*Village*	*Literacy Status*	*Participation in meeting/function*			*Total*
			Alone	*With men or women from the same or other family*	*Others*	
Meghalaya	Ringkseh	Illiterate	2	0	0	
		< Madhyamik	14	1	0	20
		> Madhyamik	3	0	0	
	Kyton-u-Mon	Illiterate	15	1	0	
		< Madhyamik	5	1	2	28
		> Madhyamik	4	0	0	
	Total	Illiterate	17	1	0	
		< Madhyamik	19	2	2	48
		> Madhyamik	7	0	0	
Tripura	Beltali	Illiterate	4	0	9	
		< Madhyamik	1	0	5	19
		> Madhyamik	0	0	0	
	Kalitila	Illiterate	5	1	3	
		< Madhyamik	5	0	4	18
		> Madhyamik	0	0	0	
	Total	Illiterate	9	1	12	
		< Madhyamik	6	0	9	37
		> Madhyamik	0	0	0	
Grand Total		Illiterate	26	2	12	
		< Madhyamik	25	2	11	85
		> Madhyamik	7	0	0	

Participation in a Meeting/Function Outside the Village

Despite the advancement made by the Indians in various aspects of modern day life, a huge chunk of them, especially those who are rural inhabitants, continue to follow their traditional cultural trends and social norms, most of which are guided by religious dogmas and the prevalent social traditions. In most places in our country, while the men remain outside the purview of the age-old customs and traditions, the women continue to be overruled by the conservative religious and social statutes. However, there have been drastic changes in the basic living condition of Indian males and females in recent years.

In the context of present day India, what is the distribution of the female household heads in the sample villages in the two north-eastern States of Meghalaya and Tripura, where the survey has been undertaken, in respect of their participation in meetings and suchlike programmes outside their villages? Table 7.24 represents the researchers' findings regarding the participation of the female heads in meetings/functions outside the village.

An important finding made by the study team is that in both the States, the literacy status of the female household heads did not impact much on their participation in meetings and functions outside the village. This fact unfolds itself in Table 7.24, which clarifies that while in Ringkseh more number of literate female heads participated in meetings and functions outside their villages all alone by themselves, in Kyton-u-Mon more illiterate females were reported to have participated in suchlike meetings outside the village, unaccompanied by their husbands or any other family member.

Similarly, in Beltali in Tripura, out of the 5 female heads who participated alone in meetings outside the village, 4 were illiterate and only 1 was literate. On the other hand, in Kalitila, out of the 6 illiterate women who picked up courage to participate in meetings outside the village, only 1 went accompanied by a family member while 5 went alone. Another 5 female heads in Kalitila who joined in such kinds of meetings were literate.

From Table 7.24 we could also infer that the social position of the females in the two villages of Meghalaya is much higher than that of the females of Tripura. That is why in Ringkseh, for instance, 19 female household heads out of the total 20 female household heads reportedly participated alone in all meetings/functions, without the prior permission of the male members of their family. In Kyton-u-Mon the above proportion was found to be 24 out of 28 female household heads.

In Tripura State, particularly in Beltali village, 5 female household heads out of the total of 19 confirmed that they participated alone in a meeting/function, and that too, without the prior permission of the male members. In Kalitila village, on the other hand, the above proportion is 10 out of a total 18 female household heads.

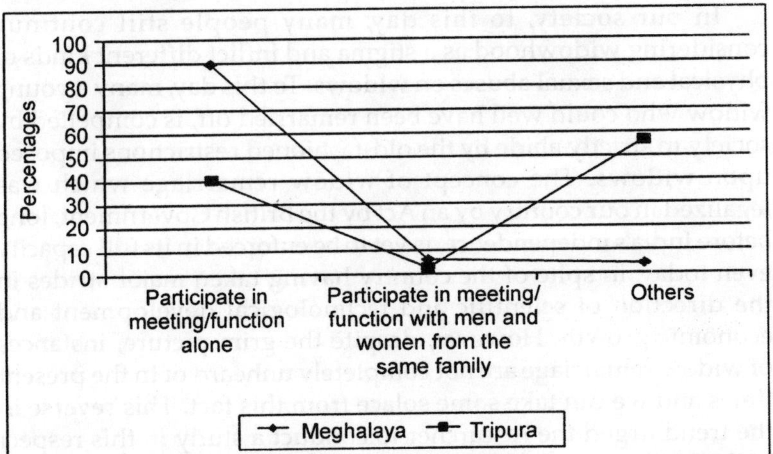

Fig. 7.46: Distribution of the Female Household Heads according to Participation in any Meeting/Function outside the Village

Thus from the above discussion we may arrive at this conclusion that Meghalaya's women are more advanced and progressive than Tripura's women, regarding their participation in meetings/functions, without the permission of the male members of their family (Fig. 7.46).

Remarriage among the Females after Husband's Death

Despite the government ruling declaring that the marriageable age of girls is eighteen years, marrying off girls much earlier and before they are physically strong to withstand the consequences of marriage and mentally steady enough to comprehend the meaning and responsibilities of marriage, is a trend in our country that is prevalent even today. And often, the age difference between the groom and the bride is very marked, with many of the grooms being twice double the age of the girls they marry. Though in the past the frequency of young girls becoming widows was more, we cannot rule out such possibilities in the present times too, despite the fact that the average life span of people has increased owing to many factors. For, many husbands meet with sudden deaths owing to sudden health complications, accidents, suicides and multitude of other reasons. So we still come across many young widows in our society, especially in the rural areas.

In our society, to this day, many people still continue considering widowhood as a stigma and inflict different kinds of physical and sexual abuses on widows. To this day, many a young widow who could well have been remarried off, is compelled by society to strictly abide by the old-fashioned restrictions imposed upon widows. The concept of widow remarriage which was legalized in our country by an Act by the British Government, long before India's independence, is yet to be enforced in its full capacity even today, in spite of the country having taken major strides in the direction of scientific and technological development and economic growth. However, despite the grim picture, instances of widow remarriage are not completely unheard of in the present times and we can take some solace from this fact. This reverse in the trend urged the researcher to conduct a study in this respect in the study area. Table 7.25 reveals in details the findings of the researchers in the sample villages in Meghalaya and Tripura.

To find out the prevalence of remarriage after husband's death among the female household heads and also their own views on widow remarriage, the researchers visited all the female-headed households for a satisfactory answer.

It was found (Table 7.25) in Tripura that a greater proportion of the women (86.48%) supported the idea that a woman should marry after her husband's death. While 6 female heads—comprising 16.21 per cent of the total female heads in the villages of Tripura, declined to make any comment on the issue, there was a lone case who did not agree with the concept of widow remarriage.

Interestingly, in Meghalaya, which has a predominantly matrilineal social frame, the number of female heads (16) who agreed with this idea of remarriage of widows was almost on the

Table 7.25: Distribution of the Female-Headed Households where Remarriage after Husband's Death is being considered

State	*Village*	*Literacy Status*	*Should marry after her husband's death*				*Total*
			Agree	*Not agree*	*Not sure*	*No comments*	
Meghalaya	Ringkseh	Illiterate	1	0	1	0	20
		<Madhyamik	5	6	3	1	
		>Madhyamik	1	0	2	0	
	Kyton-u-Mon	Illiterate	5	6	5	0	28
		<Madhyamik	2	1	5	0	
		>Madhyamik	2	0	2	0	
	Total	Illiterate	6	6	6	0	48
		<Madhyamik	7	7	8	1	
		>Madhyamik	3	0	4	0	
Tripura	Beltali	Illiterate	11	1	0	1	19
		<Madhyamik	6	0	0	0	
		>Madhyamik	0	0	0	0	
	Kalitila	Illiterate	6	0	2	1	18
		<Madhyamik	9	0	0	0	
		>Madhyamik	0	0	0	0	
	Total	Illiterate	17	1	2	2	37
		<Madhyamik	15	0	0	0	
		>Madhyamik	0	0	0	0	
Grand Total		Illiterate	23	7	8	2	85
		<Madhyamik	22	7	8	1	
		>Madhyamik	3	0	4	0	

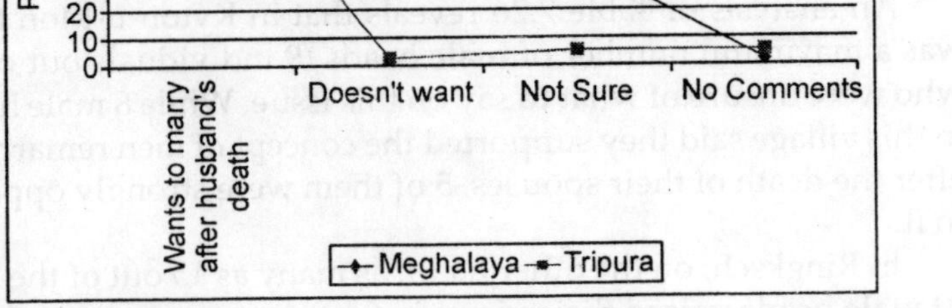

Fig. 7.47: Distribution of the Female Household Heads on the basis of Consideration about Remarriage after Husband's Death

heels of the number of female heads (13) who did not agree. However, one encouraging fact that emerged is that a considerable proportion of the female heads in Meghalaya, who are in favour of women remarrying after the death of their husbands, are literate at least up to the Madhyamik stage.

Another point to be noted here in the context of the literacy status of the female heads in Tripura is that though the State's literacy rate is higher than that of Meghalaya, in the surveyed areas, most of the female heads are either illiterate or have only primary level education (less than Madhyamik). And yet they have favoured the remarriage of widows after the death of their husbands. Contrastingly, in the surveyed areas of Meghalaya, the female heads are literate, with a few having done their matriculation too. And yet most of them are not in favour of widows marrying after their husbands' death, though the tendency is known to improve with academic achievement.

From the above observation we may arrive at this conclusion that though the females in Tripura are not much educated, yet they are far more conscious of their social and economic conditions and hence are in favour of widow remarriage after husband's death. Another pertinent implication is that the widows in the Khasi society are more self-sufficient and independent (Fig. 7.47).

Remarriage among the Males after Wife's Death

Just like the researchers made an attempt to find out the viewpoints of the female household heads on the remarriage of widows, they even knocked at the doors of the male-headed household to learn about their opinions on the remarriage of the males after the expiry of spouse. The findings are being discussed hereafter on the basis of the data represented in Table 7.26.

An analysis of Table 7.26 reveals that in Kyton-u-Mon there was a maximum number of male heads (9 individuals out of 25) who were unsure of what to say on this issue. While 8 male heads in this village said they supported the concept of men remarrying after the death of their spouses, 5 of them were strongly opposed to it.

In Ringkseh, on the other hand, as many as 15 out of the total 22 male heads voiced their views in favour of remarriage of men after the death of the spouses. An equal number of male heads

Table 7.26: Distribution of the Male-Headed Households where Remarriage after Wife's Death is being considered

State	*Village*	*Literacy Status*	*Should marry after his wife's death*				*Total*
			Agree	*Not agree*	*Not sure*	*No comments*	
Meghalaya	Ringkseh	Illiterate	0	0	1	0	25
		<Madhyamik	9	2	4	0	
		>Madhyamik	6	3	0	0	
	Kyton-u-Mon	Illiterate	3	1	2	0	22
		<Madhyamik	3	2	6	0	
		>Madhyamik	2	2	1	0	
	Total	Illiterate	3	1	3	0	47
		<Madhyamik	12	4	10	0	
		>Madhyamik	8	5	1	0	
Tripura	Beltali	Illiterate	4	1	0	0	36
		<Madhyamik	22	5	0	1	
		>Madhyamik	3	0	0	0	
	Kalitila	Illiterate	4	0	0	1	36
		<Madhyamik	20	1	1	0	
		>Madhyamik	7	1	0	1	
	Total	Illiterate	8	1	1	1	72
		<Madhyamik	42	6	1	1	
		>Madhyamik	10	0	0	1	
Grand Total		Illiterate	11	2	4	1	119
		<Madhyamik	54	10	11	1	
		>Madhyamik	18	5	1	1	

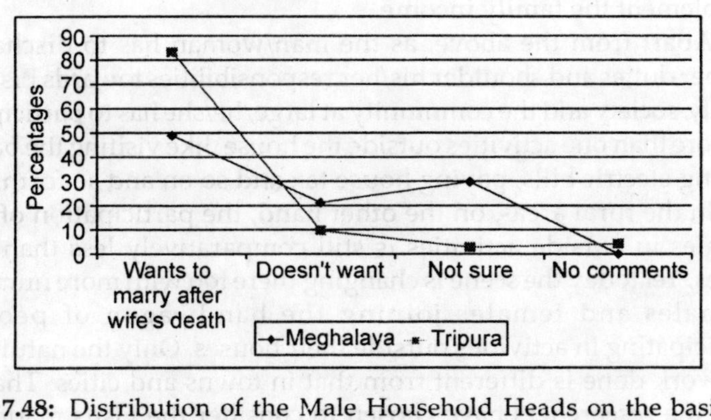

Fig. 7.48: Distribution of the Male Household Heads on the basis of Consideration about Remarriage after Wife's Death

either did not support the concept or were unsure about what to say. The two villages taken together, less than 50 per cent of the male heads supported the concept of remarriage among men.

In Tripura, a maximum proportion of the male household heads support the idea that a man should remarry after his wife's death. 29 out of 36 male heads in Beltali village, which is approximately 81 per cent of the total number of male heads in Beltali, ruled in favour of remarriage among men after the death of their spouse. In the same way, 31 out of 36 male heads (i.e. 86.11%), in Kalitila agreed with the proposition that men may remarry after widowhood.

Importantly, in both the States, a maximum of the male heads who supported the remarriage of widowers were literate at least up to the Madhyamik level.

From our findings we could infer that the male heads, in most cases, were more dependent on their spouses, if not for economic reasons, at least for home-making, which is why they have been supporting the concept of remarriage of widowers (Fig. 7.48).

Participation in Outside Activities

With life becoming more and more fast and demanding, men and women are both required to be more participative in activities other than their routine work, whether in the rural areas or in the urban. Indeed, in a town or city, a man has to get engaged in some money earning services or businesses for earning a livelihood. Today many city women are also doing some or the other kind of job to supplement the family income.

Apart from the above, as the man/woman has to discharge his/her duties and shoulder his/her responsibilities towards his/her family, society and the community at large, he/she has to participate in more than one activities outside the house, like visiting the bank, paying electric bills, paying house tax and so on and so forth.

In the rural areas, on the other hand, the participation of the females in outside activities is still comparatively less than the males. Yet today the scene is changing there too with more number of males and females joining the bandwagon of people participating in activities outside their houses. Only the nature of the work done is different from that in towns and cities. That is why the researchers have chosen to consider the visits made by the sample population to the Panchayat, Panchayat Samity, Block Office, Gram Sansad, etc., as the indices of their outside activities.

Table 7.27(a) unfolds the distribution of the household heads in the four villages located within Meghalaya and Tripura by their participation in a few named out-of-door activities.

According to Table 7.27(a), in Meghalaya, "visiting the Panchayat" was the single dominant outside activity for the male and female household heads. 80.85 per cent male heads and 83.33 per cent female heads in the two villages herein visited the Panchayat regularly. It can also been seen that 12.76 per cent of all the male heads and 12.5 per cent of all the female heads visited both the Panchayat and the Block Office. The participation of the villages' household heads in the activities of the Block Office and Panchayat Samity is negligible.

In Tripura, it was quite disheartening to realize that despite their literacy status and political consciousness, only 18.06 per cent of the male heads and 48.64 per cent of the female heads said that they participated in the activities of the Panchayat regularly. Thus, compared to the sample population in Meghalaya, Tripura reflects a poorer shade of the participation of its household heads in the activities of the Panchayat.

Again, only 12.5 per cent of the male heads and 8.10 per cent of the female heads confirmed their participation in the activities of the Panchayat and Block Office. None of the respondents in either Beltali or Kalitila visited the Block Office exclusively. However, unlike in Meghalaya, there were several respondents (29.17% male heads) in the villages in Tripura who confirmed that they participated in the activities of the Panchayat, Panchayat Samity, Zilla Parishad, Block Office, Gram Sabha and Gram Sansad.

If we consider both these States together, then it would be found that the maximum number of household heads (109 out of 204 households) paid a routine visit to the Panchayat, whenever possible. An encouraging point that caught the study team's attention in this context is that more numbers of the female heads were actually discarding their traditional conservative outlook and venturing out of their so far closed life to adjust with the changing needs and demands of the times. That is why as many as 68.23 per cent female heads from the sample villages in both the States reported that they visited the Panchayat regularly.

Table 7.27(a): Distribution of the Household Heads by their Participation in Out-of-Door Activities

State	Village	Sex	Participation																		Sub Total	Total
			None	Visit Panchayat	Visit Panchayat Samity	Visit Block Office	Visit Panchayat+ Block Office	Visit Panchayat+Panchayat Samity	Visit Panchayat+Zilla Parishad	Panchayat+Panchayat Samity+Block Office	Panchayat+ Zilla Parishad+ Block Office	Panchayat+Gram Sabha+Gram Sansad	Panchayat+ Panchayat Samity+Zilla Parishad+Block Office	Panchayat+ Panchayat Samity+Gram Sabha+Block Office	Panchayat+ Panchayat Samity+Gram Sabha+Gram Sansad	Panchayat+ Zilla Parishad+Block Office+Gram Sabha	Panchayat+Block Office+Gram Sansad+Gram Sabha	Panchayat+Panchayat Samity+Zilla Parishad+Block Office+Gram Sabha	Panchayat+Panchayat Samity+ Block Office+Gram Sabha+Gram Sansad	Panchayat+Panchayat Samity+Zilla Parishad+Block Office+Gram Sabha+ Gram Sansad		
(1)	(2)	(3)	(4)	(5)	(6)	(7)	(8)	(9)	(10)	(11)	(12)	(13)	(14)	(15)	(16)	(17)	(18)	(19)	(20)	(21)	(22)	(23)
Meghalaya	Ringkseh	Male	2	21	0	1	1	0	0	0	0	0	0	0	0	0	0	0	0	0	25	45
		Female	0	19	1	0	0	0	0	0	0	0	0	0	0	0	0	0	0	0	20	

(Contd.)

Table 7.27(a) — *Contd.*

(1)	(2)	(3)	(4)	(5)	(6)	(7)	(8)	(9)	(10)	(11)	(12)	(13)	(14)	(15)	(16)	(17)	(18)	(19)	(20)	(21)	(22)	(23)
	Kyton-u-Mon	Male	0	17	0	0	5	0	0	0	0	0	0	0	0	0	0	0	0	0	22	50
		Female	0	21	0	1	6	0	0	0	0	0	0	0	0	0	0	0	0	0	28	
	Total	Male	2	38	0	1	6	0	0	0	0	0	0	0	0	0	0	0	0	0	47	95
		Female	0	40	1	1	6	0	0	0	0	0	0	0	0	0	0	0	0	0	48	
Tripura	Beltali	Male	1	6	0	0	2	2	1	0	0	3	2	0	1	0	0	0	2	16	36	55
		Female	0	10	0	0	2	1	0	1	1	0	1	1	1	0	0	0	1	0	19	
	Kalitila	Male	4	7	0	0	7	0	0	3	0	4	2	0	1	1	1	1	0	5	36	54
		Female	2	8	0	0	1	0	0	1	0	1	0	1	0	0	0	0	1	3	18	
	Total	Male	5	13	0	0	9	2	1	3	0	7	4	0	2	1	1	1	2	21	72	109
		Female	2	18	0	0	3	1	0	2	1	1	1	2	1	0	0	0	2	3	37	
Grand Total		Male	7	51	0	1	15	2	1	3	0	7	4	0	2	1	1	1	2	21	119	204
		Female	2	58	1	1	9	1	0	2	1	1	1	2	1	0	0	0	2	3	85	
		Total	9	109	1	2	24	3	1	5	1	8	5	2	3	1	1	1	4	24	204	

Table 7.27(b): Distribution of the Counterparts of the Household Heads by their Participation in Out-of-Door Activities

State	Village	Sex	Participation														Sub-total	Total
			None	Visit Panchayat	Visit Panchayat+Panchayat Samity	Visit Panchayat+Z illa Parishad	Visit Panchayat+ Block Office	Panchayat+Gram Sabha	Panchayat+Panchayat Samity+Block Office	Panchayat+Gram Sabha+Gram Sansad	Panchayat+ Panchayat Samity+Zilla Parishad+Block Office	Panchayat+ Panchayat Samity+Gram Sabha+Block Office	Panchayat+ Panchayat Samity+Gram Sabha+Gram Sansad	Panchayat+Panchayat Samity+ Block Office+Gram Sabha+Gram Sansad	Panchayat +Zilla Parishad+Block Office+Gram Sabha+ Gram Sansad	Panchayat+Panchayat Samity+Zilla Parishad+Block Office+Gram Sabha+ Gram Sansad	Panchayaty+Zilla Parishad+Gram Sabha+ Gram Sansad		
(1)	(2)	(3)	(4)	(5)	(6)	(6)	(7)	(8)	(9)	(9)	(10)	(11)	(12)	(13)	(14)	(15)	(16)	(17)	(18)
Meghalaya	Ringkseh	Male	0	15	0	0	1	0	0	0	0	0	0	0	0	0	0	16	35
		Female	0	19	0	0	0	0	0	0	0	0	0	0	0	0	0	19	
	Kyton-u-Mon	Male	0	16	0	0	4	0	0	0	0	0	0	0	0	0	0	20	41
		Female	0	17	0	0	4	0	0	0	0	0	0	0	0	0	0	21	
	Total	Male	0	31	0	0	5	0	0	0	0	0	0	0	0	0	0	36	76
		Female	0	36	0	0	4	0	0	0	0	0	0	0	0	0	0	40	
Tripura	Beltali	Male	0	4	0	1	0	1	0	0	3	0	0	0	0	7	1	17	53
		Female	10	10	2	0	2	0	2	3	0	1	2	2	0	2	0	36	

(Contd.)

(1)	(2)	(3)	(4)	(5)	(6)	(6)	(7)	(8)	(9)	(9)	(10)	(11)	(12)	(13)	(14)	(15)	(16)	(17)	(18)
	Kalitila	Male	0	0	0	0	2	0	4	1	0	2	0	0	2	2	1	14	50
		Female	10	16	3	1	2	0	1	2	0	0	0	0	0	1	0	36	
	Total	Male	0	4	0	1	2	1	4	1	3	2	0	0	2	9	2	31	103
		Female	20	26	5	1	4	0	3	5	0	1	2	2	0	3	0	72	
Grand Total		Male	0	35	0	1	7	1	4	1	3	2	0	0	2	9	2	67	179
		Female	20	62	5	1	8	0	3	5	0	1	2	2	0	3	0	112	
		Total	20	97	5	2	15	1	7	6	3	3	2	2	2	12	2	179	

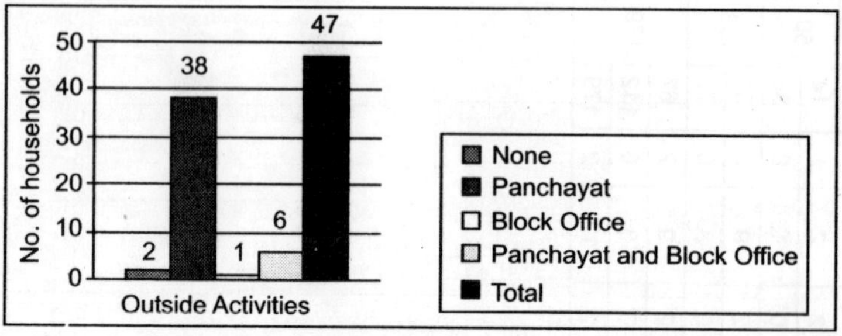

Fig. 7.49: Distribution of the Male Household Heads in Meghalaya based on Participation in Outside Activities

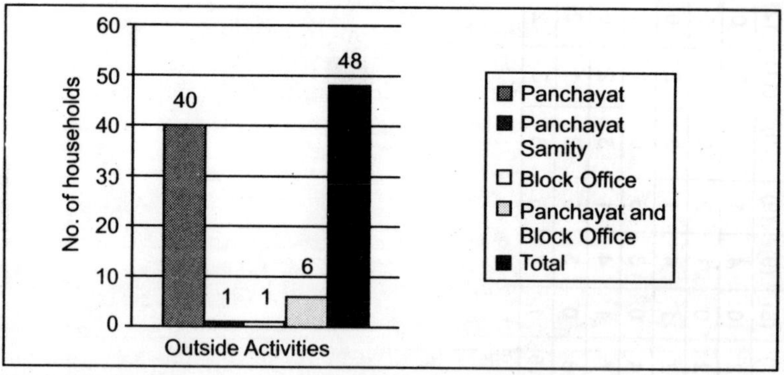

Fig. 7.50: Distribution of the Female Household Heads in Meghalaya based on Participation in Outside Activities

The above result for the village household heads in Tripura and Meghalaya also holds good for the counterparts of the household heads in these States. Table 7.27(b) confirms the stated claims (Figs. 7.49 to 7.52).

(E) CULTURAL EMPOWERMENT

Cultural empowerment means the power to improve upon one's mind, manners, taste, etc., by engaging the psyche and physique in some cultural activities, which are over and above the mundane everyday activities of life. The ideas, customs, skills, arts, etc., of a given people in a given period combines to give us the culture of the people of that region.

As is the trend in today's world, apart from the regular

everyday activities of daily living, people mostly prefer to read the newspaper, listen to radio programmes and watch television programmes. The sample population was also interviewed for knowing whether or not they were culturally empowered to pursue these activities. Tables 7.28(a), 7.28(b), 7.29(a), 7.29(b) 7.30(a) and 7.30(b) help us form an idea about the popularity of activities like reading the newspaper, listening to the radio and watching television in the sample villages.

Table 7.28(a) shows the distribution of the male and female household heads in the sample villages by their practice of reading the newspaper.

So far as the picture for the villages in Meghalaya is available, we see that 9 out of 20 female household heads and 12 out of 25 male household heads in Ringkseh village made it a point to read the newspaper everyday. Together these household heads comprise 46.67 per cent of the total household heads in Ringkseh. In Kyton-u-Mon, 8 males comprising 36.36 per cent of the male heads and 8 females comprising 28.57 per cent of the female heads read the point everyday.

While 37.95 per cent of all the household heads in Ringkseh and Kyton-u-Mon together read the newspaper daily, 28.42 per cent said that they never read the newspaper and 32.63 per cent said they read the newspaper but not everyday.

Surprisingly, the popularity of newspaper reading as a regular activity is not noticed in the two villages of Tripura, where only 15.27 per cent of the total male household heads and 5.4 per cent female household heads have confirmed that they read the newspaper customarily. 36.11 per cent male heads, however, said that they read the newspaper but not everyday as they did not find the time to sit with it. 8.10 per cent female heads agreed that they read the newspaper occasionally as and when possible for them.

Exactly 48.61 per cent of the male heads in both the villages in Tripura confirmed that they never read the newspaper. Considered in the background of their literacy status, 69.44 per cent of this latter group that never read the newspaper, were literate.

Among the female heads in Tripura, 86.84 per cent nodded in the negative when they were asked if or not they read the newspaper.

From all of the above we realize that there is still enough scope for pursuing newspaper reading as a cultural activity; hence, efforts

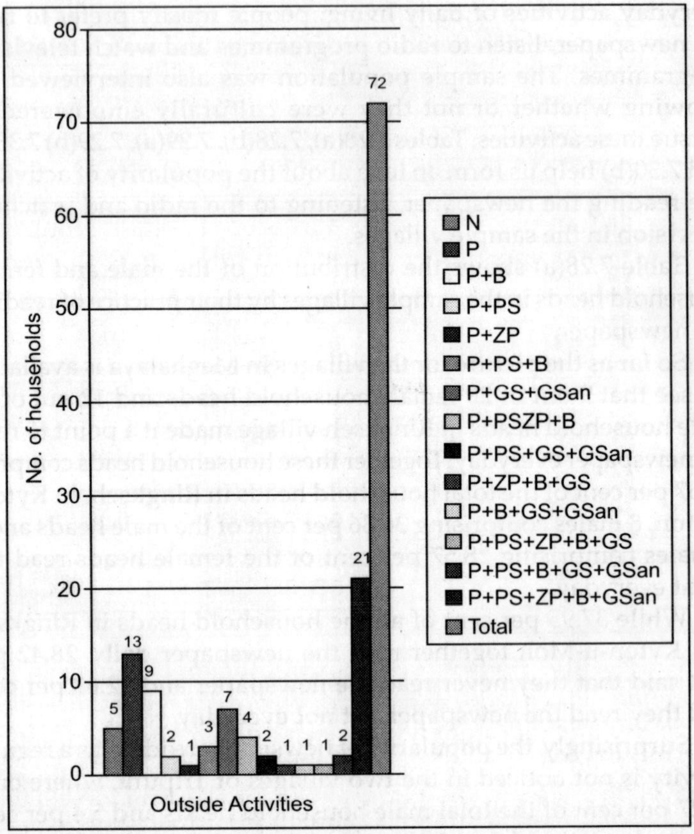

Fig. 7.51: Distribution of the Male Household Heads in Tripura based on Participation in Outside Activities

should next be driven to raise the consciousness of the people, especially those among them who are literate, to cultivate the practice of newspaper-reading in order to be more aware of the happenings in the world around.

According to Table 7.28(b), which brings out the distribution of the counterparts of the household heads in the sample villages by their practice of reading newspaper, less than one-third, i.e., 29.85 per cent of all the male counterparts and 15.18 per cent of all the female counterparts read the newspaper regularly. Between Ringkseh and Kyton-u-Mon, the male and female counterparts of Ringkseh were more culturally empowered in respect of reading

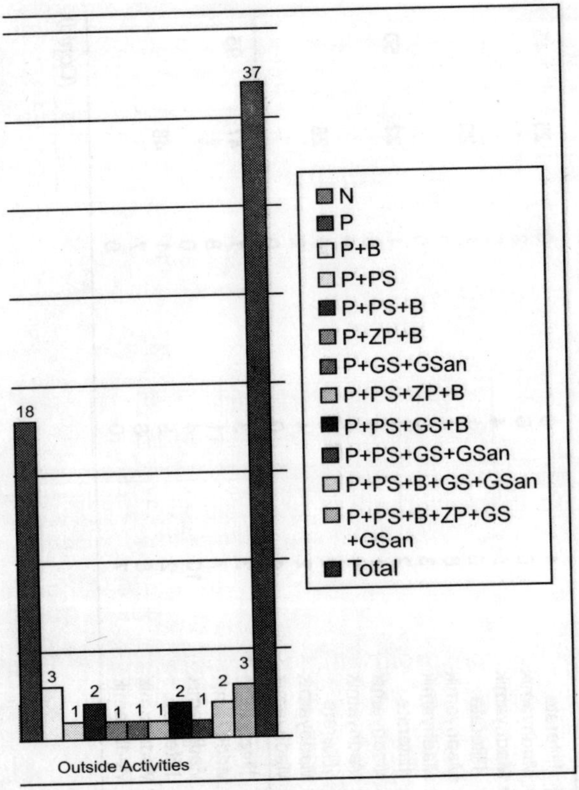

Note: N—None, P—Panchayat, ZP—Zilla Parishad, B—Block Office, GS—Gram Sabha, GSan—Gram Sansad

Fig. 7.52: Distribution of the Female Household Heads in Tripura based on Participation in Outside Activities

the newspaper on a regular basis, as 62.85 per cent of them pursued this activity routinely, come what may. Whereas, in Kyton-u-Mon, only 24.39 per cent of all the counterparts engaged their time in newspaper reading.

Just like among the household heads, the scene in Tripura is not at all encouraging even among the counterparts of the household heads, in respect of their preference for newspaper reading, as only 4.85 per cent of them said that they were habituated to reading the newspaper regularly while 69.90 per cent admitted that they never read the newspaper. 25.24 per cent made it clear that they did not find it obligatory to read the

Table 7.28(a): Distribution of the Household Heads by their Practice of Reading Newspaper

State	*Village*	*Sex*	*Literacy Status*	*Read Newspaper*		*Never*	*Sub total*	*Total*
				Everyday	*Not Everyday*			
Meghalaya	Ringkseh	Male	Illiterate	1	0	0	25	45
			< Madhyamik	6	6	3		
			> Madhyamik	5	4	0		
		Female	Illiterate	0	1	1	20	
			< Madhyamik	6	4	5		
			> Madhyamik	3	0	0		
	Kyton-u-Mon	Male	Illiterate	2	3	1	22	50
			< Madhyamik	1	5	5		
			> Madhyamik	5	0	0		
		Female	Illiterate	2	4	10	28	
			< Madhyamik	2	4	2		
			> Madhyamik	4	0	0		
	Total	Male	Illiterate	3	3	1	47	95
			< Madhyamik	7	11	8		
			> Madhyamik	10	4	0		
		Female	Illiterate	2	5	11	48	
			< Madhyamik	8	8	7		
			> Madhyamik	7	0	0		

(Contd).

Table 7.28 (a)— *Contd.*

State	Village	Sex	Literacy Status	Read Newspaper			Sub Total	Total
				Everyday	Not Everyday	Never		
Tripura	Beltali	Male	Illiterate	0	0	5	36	55
			< Madhyamik	2	11	15		
			> Madhyamik	2	1	0		
		Female	Illiterate	0	0	13	19	
			< Madhyamik	1	0	5		
			> Madhyamik	0	0	0		
	Kalitila	Male	Illiterate	0	0	5	36	54
			< Madhyamik	2	11	9		
			> Madhyamik	5	3	1		
		Female	Illiterate	0	0	9	18	
			< Madhyamik	1	3	5		
			> Madhyamik	0	0	0		
	Total	Male	Illiterate	0	0	10	72	109
			< Madhyamik	4	22	24		
			> Madhyamik	7	4	1		
		Female	Illiterate	0	0	22	37	
			< Madhyamik	2	3	10		
			> Madhyamik	0	0	0		
Grand Total				50	60	94		204

Table 7.28(b): Distribution of the Counterparts of the Household Heads by their Practice of Reading Newspaper

State	*Village*	*Sex*	*Read Newspaper*			*Sub Total*	*Total*
			Everyday	*Not Everyday*	*Never*		
Meghalaya	Ringkseh	Male	10	2	4	16	35
		Female	12	7	0	19	
	Kyton-u-Mon	Male	6	5	9	20	41
		Female	4	9	8	21	
	Total	Male	16	7	13	36	76
		Female	16	16	8	40	
Tripura	Beltali	Male	1	8	8	17	53
		Female	0	7	29	36	
	Kalitila	Male	3	5	6	14	50
		Female	1	6	29	36	
	Total	Male	4	13	14	31	103
		Female	1	13	58	72	
Grand Total		Male	20	20	27	67	179
		Female	17	29	66	112	

newspaper everyday, obviously due to some or the other inconveniences (Fig. 7.53).

Based on the data provided in Table 7.29(a), the per cent-wise distribution of the male heads in Ringkseh in Meghalaya, who listened to the radio everyday, listened to it occasionally and never listened to it are 36 per cent, 40 per cent and 24 per cent respectively. Among the female heads this distribution goes as 30 per cent, 25 per cent and 45 per cent respectively. A comparison between the two shows that listening to the radio was more frequent among the male heads than among the female heads. This is an indication of the fact that the males found more time to spare for pursuing this activity.

The situation in Kyton-u-Mon was also similar, though here the male household heads (22.72%) registered a comparatively narrower lead over the female household heads (21.43%) in so far as listening to the radio is concerned.

Table 7.29(a): Distribution of the Household Heads by their Preference for Listening to the Radio

State	Village	Sex	Literacy Status	Listen Radio			Sub Total	Total
				Everyday	Not Everyday	Never		
Meghalaya	Ringkseh	Male	Illiterate	1	0	0	25	45
			< Madhyamik	3	7	5		
			> Madhyamik	5	3	1		
		Female	Illiterate	0	0	2	20	
			< Madhyamik	3	5	7		
			> Madhyamik	3	0	0		
	Kyton-u-Mon	Male	Illiterate	1	1	4	22	50
			< Madhyamik	1	5	5		
			> Madhyamik	3	2	0		
		Female	Illiterate	2	2	12	28	
			< Madhyamik	2	4	2		
			> Madhyamik	2	1	1		
	Total	Male	Illiterate	2	1	4	47	95
			< Madhyamik	4	12	10		
			> Madhyamik	8	5	1		
		Female	Illiterate	2	2	14	48	
			< Madhyamik	5	9	9		
			> Madhyamik	5	1	1		

(Contd.)

Table 7.29 (a) (*Contd.*)

State	*Village*	*Sex*	*Literacy Status*	*Listen Radio*			*Sub Total*	*Total*
				Everyday	*Not Everyday*	*Never*		
Tripura	Beltali	Male	Illiterate	0	0	5	36	55
			< Madhyamik	3	9	16		
			> Madhyamik	1	1	1		
		Female	Illiterate	0	2	11	19	
			< Madhyamik	0	1	5		
			> Madhyamik	0	0	0		
	Kalitila	Male	Illiterate	0	0	5	36	54
			< Madhyamik	1	3	18		
			> Madhyamik	0	4	5		
		Female	Illiterate	0	1	8	18	
			< Madhyamik	0	0	9		
			> Madhyamik	0	0	0		
	Total	Male	Illiterate	0	0	10	72	109
			< Madhyamik	4	12	34		
			> Madhyamik	1	5	6		
		Female	Illiterate	0	3	19	37	
			< Madhyamik	0	1	14		
			> Madhyamik	0	0	0		

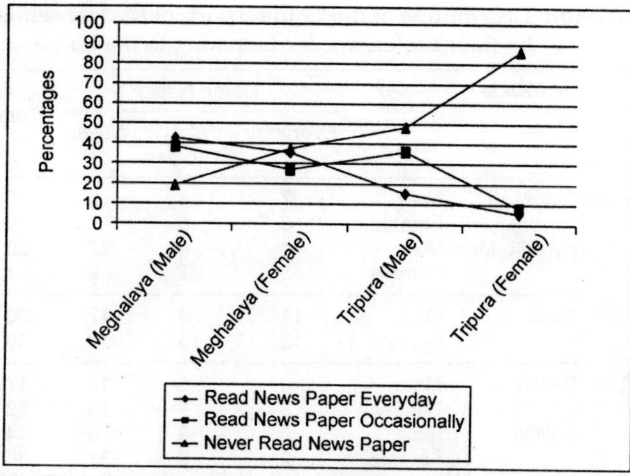

Fig. 7.53: Distribution of the Household Heads by their Practice of Reading Newspaper

It is indeed very disappointing to take a look at the figures for Tripura where as many as 83 male and female heads, accounting for 76.14 per cent of all the household heads, never listened to the radio and 19.26 per cent listened occasionally. There were just a handful of male household heads (4.58%) who confided that they listened to the radio everyday and never missed out on their favourite programmes.

According to Table 7.29(b), 30.56 per cent of all the male counterparts and 32.5 per cent of all the female counterparts in Meghalaya voiced their preference for listening to the radio everyday.

On the other hand, in Tripura, listening to the radio was a regular practice among only 6.94 per cent of the female counterparts, while none of the male counterparts followed this activity on daily basis. Still, comparing Table 7.29(a) with 7.29(b) we may say that the female counterparts in Tripura found more time for relaxation, unlike the female heads here, who had to shoulder many family responsibilities (Fig. 7.54).

So far as the household heads' preference for watching television (TV) is concerned, Table 7.30(a) shows that irrespective of their literacy status, 39.21 per cent household heads in Meghalaya and Tripura, taken together, found the required time to sit and watch TV programmes everyday, 24.01 per cent could

Table 7.29(b): Distribution of the Counterparts of the Household Heads by their Preference for Listening to the Radio

State	*Village*	*Sex*	*Listen Radio*			*Sub Total*	*Total*
			Everyday	*Not Everyday*	*Never*		
Meghalaya	Ringkseh	Male	7	4	5	16	35
		Female	8	8	3	19	
	Kyton-u-Mon	Male	4	4	12	20	41
		Female	5	7	9	21	
	Total	Male	11	8	17	36	76
		Female	13	15	12	40	
Tripura	Beltali	Male	0	5	12	17	53
		Female	3	7	26	36	
	Kalitila	Male	0	8	6	14	50
		Female	2	3	31	36	
	Total	Male	0	13	18	31	103
		Female	5	10	57	72	
Grand Total		Male	11	21	35	67	179
		Female	18	25	69	112	

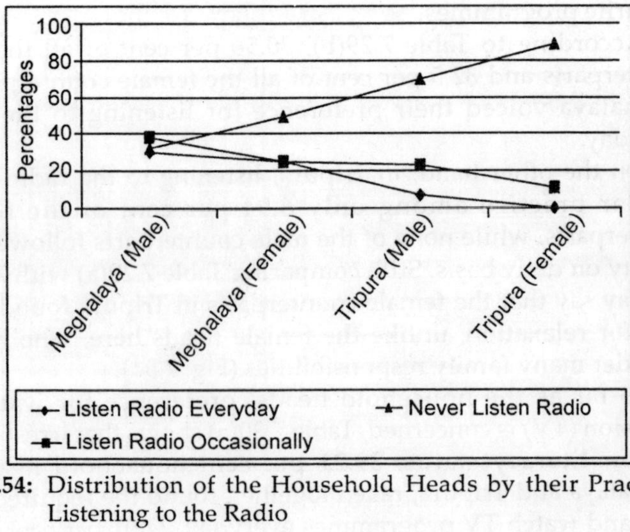

Fig. 7.54: Distribution of the Household Heads by their Practice of Listening to the Radio

Table 7.30(a): Distribution of the Household Heads by their Preference for Watching TV

State	Village	Sex	Literacy Status	Watch TV			Sub Total	Total
				Everyday	Not Everyday	Never		
Meghalaya	Ringkseh	Male	Illiterate	1	0	0	25	45
			< Madhyamik	6	2	7		
			> Madhyamik	5	3	1		
		Female	Illiterate	0	0	2	20	
			< Madhyamik	3	2	10		
			> Madhyamik	2	1	0		
	Kyton-u-Mon	Male	Illiterate	1	1	4	22	50
			< Madhyamik	3	3	5		
			> Madhyamik	3	1	1		
		Female	Illiterate	3	1	12	28	
			< Madhyamik	3	2	3		
			> Madhyamik	0	1	3		
	Total	Male	Illiterate	2	1	4	47	95
			< Madhyamik	9	5	12		
			> Madhyamik	8	4	2		
		Female	Illiterate	3	1	14	48	
			< Madhyamik	6	4	13		
			> Madhyamik	2	2	3		

(Contd.)

Table 7.30(a) — *Contd.*

State	Village	Sex	Literacy Status	Watch TV			Sub Total	Total
				Everyday	Not Everyday	Never		
Tripura	Beltali	Male	Illiterate	1	3	1	36	55
			< Madhyamik	14	10	4		
			> Madhyamik	3	0	0		
		Female	Illiterate	4	3	6	19	
			< Madhyamik	3	2	1		
			> Madhyamik	0	0	0		
	Kalitila	Male	Illiterate	1	2	2	36	54
			< Madhyamik	9	5	8		
			> Madhyamik	6	3	0		
		Female	Illiterate	2	2	5	18	
			< Madhyamik	7	2	0		
			> Madhyamik	0	0	0		
	Total	Male	Illiterate	2	5	3	72	109
			< Madhyamik	23	15	12		
			> Madhyamik	9	3	0		
		Female	Illiterate	6	5	11	37	
			< Madhyamik	10	4	1		
			> Madhyamik	0	0	0		
Grand Total				80	49	75		204

not watch TV programmes regularly and 36.76 per cent never had the opportunity to watch TV programmes.

Thus from all the Tables taken together we could conclude that between the sample population in the two States, it were the household heads from the villages of Meghalaya who cultivated the habit of reading the newspaper regularly as well as listening to the radio and watching the TV regularly. In Tripura a lesser number of the sample population indulged in any or all of the above activities.

Table 7.30(b): Distribution of the Counterparts of the Household Heads by their Preference for Watching TV

State	*Village*	*Sex*	*Watch TV*			*Sub Total*	*Total*
			Everyday	*Not Everyday*	*Never*		
Meghalaya	Ringkseh	Male	6	4	6	16	35
		Female	11	3	5	19	
	Kyton-u-Mon	Male	5	11	4	20	41
		Female	5	11	5	21	
	Total	Male	11	15	10	36	76
		Female	16	14	10	40	
Tripura	Beltali	Male	10	3	4	17	53
		Female	20	9	7	36	
	Kalitila	Male	10	2	2	14	50
		Female	21	7	8	36	
	Total	Male	20	5	6	31	103
		Female	41	16	15	72	
Grand Total		Male	31	20	16	67	179
		Female	57	30	25	112	

From Table 7.30(b) we get to learn that like the household heads themselves, their counterparts too are similarly distributed in so far as their frequency of watching TV programmes is concerned (Fig. 7.55).

Opinion about Teachers in Girls' School

Today the situation in the villages of India is much improved and coming straight to the issue, we may say that in many parts people have given their consent to let the girls participate in the education

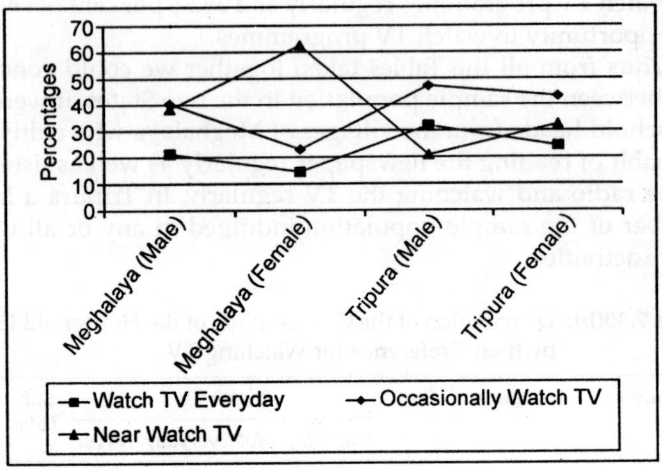

Fig. 7.55: Distribution of the Household Heads by their Practice of Watching TV

Table 7.31(a): Distribution of the Household Heads on the basis of their Opinion about the Teachers in Girls' Schools

State	*Village*	*Sex*	*Teachers in Girls School*			*Sub Total*	*Total*
			Should be Women	*Need not be Women*	*Others*		
Meghalaya	Ringkseh	Male	1	15	9	25	45
		Female	1	15	4	20	
	Kyton-u-Mon	Male	1	7	14	22	50
		Female	3	15	10	28	
	Total	Male	2	22	23	47	95
		Female	4	30	14	48	
Tripura	Beltali	Male	5	25	6	36	55
		Female	5	7	7	19	
	Kalitila	Male	1	19	16	36	54
		Female	5	8	5	18	
	Total	Male	6	44	22	72	109
		Female	10	15	12	37	
Grand Total		Male	8	66	45	119	204
		Female	14	45	26	85	

programmes being implemented by the government to improve upon literacy rates in the country. Consequently, there has been a growth in the number of girls' schools in the country and with that there has been a steady rise in the number of teachers who are recruited to these schools.

Should male teachers be allowed to work in girls' school? Do the villagers have any preferences for female teachers for their school-going daughters? These are some pertinent questions that the researchers wanted answers from the sample population during their survey in Meghalaya and Tripura. The data collected have been elaborated in Table 7.31(a).

As it gets revealed in Table 7.31(a), 30 female household heads out of 48 female household heads in the villages of Meghalaya consider it unimportant for the teachers recruited to girls' schools to be women only. Out of these 30 female heads, 21 are literate. Percentage-wise, 75 per cent and 53.57 per cent of the total female household heads in Ringkseh and Kyton-u-Mon respectively were liberal in their viewpoint on the sex of the teachers in girls' schools. The number of the sample female heads in the State who were

Table 7.31(b): Distribution of the Counterparts of the Household Heads on the basis of their Opinion about the Teachers in Girls' Schools

State	*Village*	*Sex*	*Teachers in Girls School*			*Sub Total*	*Total*
			Should be Women	*Need not be Women*	*Others*		
Meghalaya	Ringkseh	Male	0	12	4	16	35
		Female	1	16	2	19	
	Kyton-u-Mon	Male	0	8	12	20	41
		Female	2	12	7	21	
	Total	Male	0	20	16	36	76
		Female	3	28	9	40	
Tripura	Beltali	Male	2	15	0	17	53
		Female	8	25	3	36	
	Kalitila	Male	1	10	3	14	50
		Female	4	18	14	36	
	Total	Male	3	25	3	31	103
		Female	12	43	17	72	
Grand Total		Male	3	45	19	67	179
		Female	15	71	26	112	

firm in their opinion that teachers in girls' school should be females only, is negligible.

In Tripura, on the other hand, only 15 female heads out of the total 37 female heads validated that they were not bothered about the sex of the teachers in girls' schools—they might be male or female. This group accounted for 40.54 per cent of the total female heads in the sample population. 10 female heads out of the total 37 female household heads (27.02%) in Tripura voiced their opinion in favour of female teachers in girls' schools. 32.43 per cent female heads in the two villages did not make any clear comments on the issue.

In comparison to the female heads, it seems that the male household heads in both Meghalaya and Tripura are more liberal in their opinion about the teachers in the girls' schools. That is why, between the two States, there are as many as 66 male heads who confirmed that they did not worry about the sex of the teachers who taught in the girls' schools. The ratio between the male household heads in Meghalaya and Tripura, who said that the teachers in girl's school should not be necessarily women, is 1 : 1.3 [Table 7.31(b)].

If we consider the opinion of the counterparts of the household heads, then it gets noticed that the results for the household heads in general hold good for the counterparts also. However, the situation in Tripura, among the women especially, has improved significantly and today 43 female counterparts out of 72 think that they do not mind if the teachers in girls' schools are not females (Fig. 7.56 and 7.57).

Opinion about Teachers in Boys' School

The sample population in the villages were also asked their opinion about the teachers in boys' schools like—should only male teachers teach in boys' schools? Did females make better teachers, even for boys' schools? The data collected in this regard have been represented in Table 7.31(a).

Table 7.32(a) brings out the fact that, irrespective of sex, many of the household heads think that male teachers may not exclusively be appointed in boys' schools.

So, while in Meghalaya, 15 out of the 20 female household heads in Ringkseh and 15 out of the 28 female household heads in

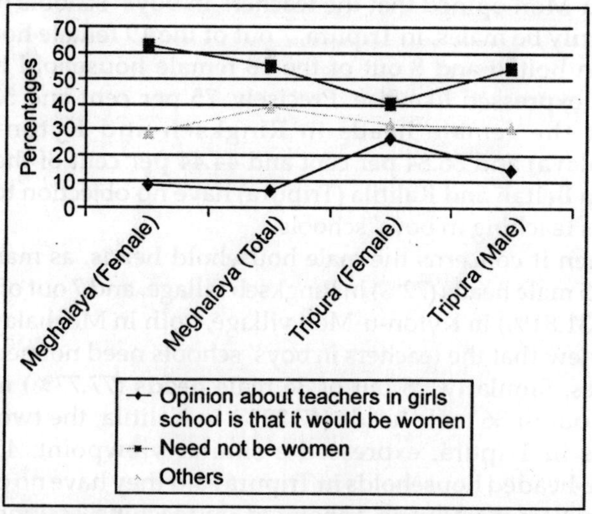

Fig. 7.56: Distribution of the Female Household Heads on the basis of their Opinion about the Teachers in Girls' School

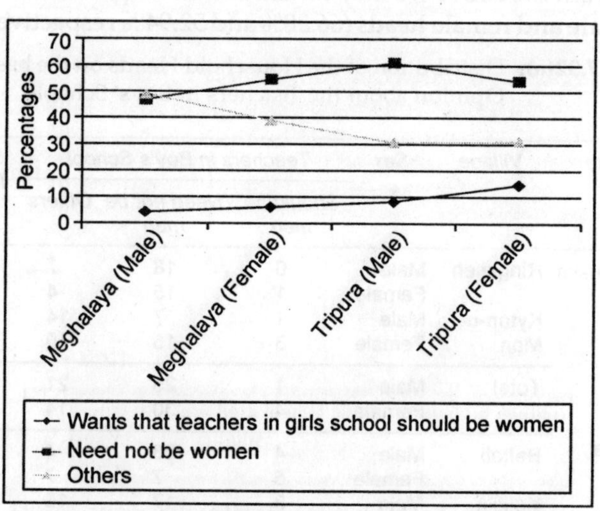

Fig. 7.57: Distribution of the Male Household Heads on the basis of their Opinion about the Teachers in Girls' School

Kyton-u-Mon opined that the teachers in boys' schools need not necessarily be males, in Tripura, 7 out of the 19 female household heads in Beltali and 8 out of the 18 female household heads in Kalitila expressed likewise. Precisely, 75 per cent and 53.57 per cent of the female heads in Ringkseh and Kyton-u-Mon (Meghalaya) and 36.84 per cent and 44.44 per cent of the female heads in Beltali and Kalitila (Tripura) have no objection to female teachers teaching in boys' schools.

When it concerns the male household heads, as many as 18 out of 25 male heads (72%) in Ringkseh village, and 7 out of 22 male heads (31.81%) in Kyton-u-Mon village, both in Meghalaya, were of the view that the teachers in boys' schools need not necessarily be males. Similarly, 28 out of 36 male heads (77.77%) in Beltali and 17 out of 36 male heads (47.22%) in Kalitila, the two sample villages in Tripura, expressed a similar viewpoint. 45 out of 72 male-headed households in Tripura said they have no objection to female teachers being appointed on teaching assignments in boys' schools.

From the above we may conclude that a significant number of the male and female heads (66.38% and 52.94% respectively) agree

Table 7.32(a): Distribution of the Household Heads on the basis of their Opinion about the Teachers in Boys' Schools

State	*Village*	*Sex*	*Teachers in Boy's School*			*Sub Total*	*Total*
			Should be men	*Need not be men*	*Others*		
Meghalaya	Ringkseh	Male	0	18	7	25	45
		Female	1	15	4	20	
	Kyton-u-Mon	Male	1	7	14	22	50
		Female	3	15	10	28	
	Total	Male	1	25	21	47	95
		Female	4	30	14	48	
Tripura	Beltali	Male	4	28	4	36	55
		Female	5	7	7	19	
	Kalitila	Male	3	17	16	36	54
		Female	5	8	5	18	
	Total	Male	7	45	20	72	109
		Female	10	15	12	37	
Grand Total		Male	8	70	41	119	204
		Female	14	45	26	85	

that female teachers make good teachers for boys' schools as well and so gender differentiation should not be made while recruiting teachers to boys' schools.

Even when we consider the counterparts of the household heads, as shown in Table 7.32(b), we see that among a majority of the counterparts in all the places, the viewpoint that teachers in boys' schools need not be males only holds good (Figs. 7.58 and 7.59).

Where Family Members Go When Sick

How adequately developed is the health infrastructure in Meghalaya and Tripura and how much aware are the people here about the existing treatment facilities available in their localities? Whom do the household heads consult when they or any of their family members is ill? Do the people have faith in modern allopathy, or do they find reliable homoeopath doctors and ayurveds in their localities? Are there hospitals or health centres near their houses? These were some pertinent questions that the

Table 7.32(b): Distribution of the Counterparts of the Household Heads on the basis of their Opinion about the Teachers in Boys' Schools

State	*Village*	*Sex*	*Teachers in Boy's School*			*Sub Total*	*Total*
			Should be men	*Need not be men*	*Others*		
Meghalaya	Ringkseh	Male	1	15	0	16	35
		Female	0	16	3	19	
	Kyton-u-Mon	Male	0	8	12	20	41
		Female	2	12	7	21	
	Total	Male	1	23	12	36	76
		Female	2	28	10	40	
Tripura	Beltali	Male	2	15	0	17	53
		Female	6	27	3	36	
	Kalitila	Male	2	9	3	14	50
		Female	5	17	14	36	
	Total	Male	4	24	3	31	103
		Female	11	44	17	72	
Grand Total		Male	5	47	15	67	179
		Female	13	72	27	112	

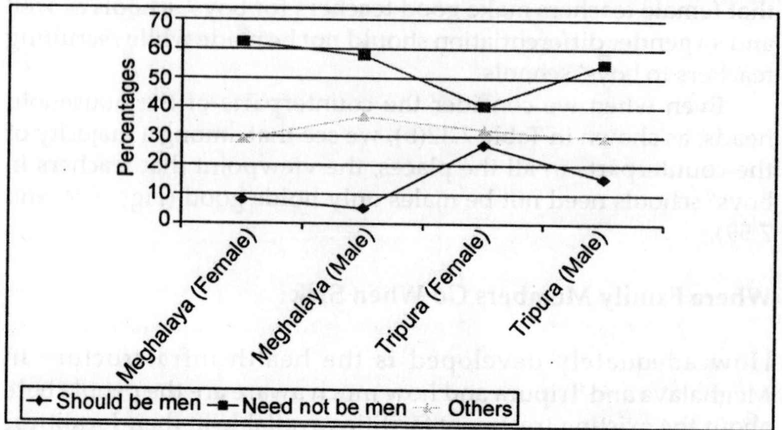

Fig. 7.58: Distribution of the Female Household Heads on the basis of their Opinion about the Teachers in Boys' School

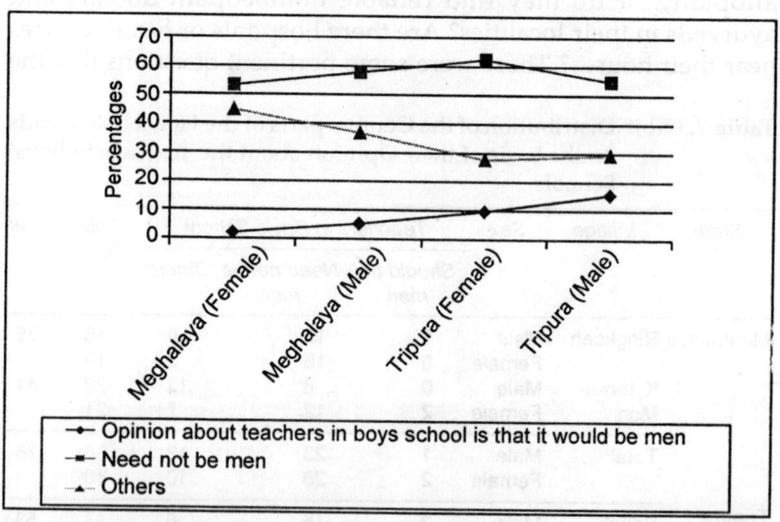

Fig. 7.59: Distribution of Male-Headed Households on their Opinion about the Teachers in Boys School

study team wanted to find about. And so the representative household heads too were questioned accordingly. Table 7.33 reveals the data collected in this regard.

From Table 7.33 it is evident that in maximum cases, when the household heads in the sample villages or any of their family members fall sick, they go for treatment to an MBBS doctor.

Table 7.33: Distribution of the Households by Place where Family Members go for Treatment during Sickness

State	Village	Sex	Go for treatment during sickness										Sub-Total	Total
			Hospital	PHC	MBBS Doctor	Health Worker	Kaviraj	MBBS Doctor+Hospital	Homoeopath+ MBBS Doctor+Hospital	Kaviraj+ MBBS Doctor+Hospital	Kaviraj/Homoeopath/ Health Worker/MBBS Doctor/PHC/Hospital	NA		
Meghalaya	Ringkseh	Male	1	0	10	0	1	9	0	0	1	3	25	45
		Female	2	0	2	1	0	8	0	0	7	0	20	
	Kyton-u-Mor	Male	0	0	7	0	0	2	0	9	4	0	22	50
		Female	0	0	11	0	0	5	0	6	5	1	28	
	Total	Male	1	0	17	0	1	11	0	9	5	3	47	95
		Female	2	0	13	1	0	13	0	6	12	1	48	
Tripura	Beltali	Male	25	1	1	0	0	8	0	0	1	0	36	55
		Female	14	0	1	0	0	2	0	0	0	2	19	
	Kalitila	Male	18	0	0	0	0	14	2	0	1	1	36	54
		Female	9	0	0	0	0	5	0	1	2	1	18	
	Total	Male	43	1	1	0	0	22	2	0	2	1	72	109
		Female	23	0	1	0	0	7	0	1	2	3	37	
Grand Total		Male	44	1	18	0	1	33	2	9	7	4	119	204
		Female	25	0	14	1	0	20	0	7	14	4	85	

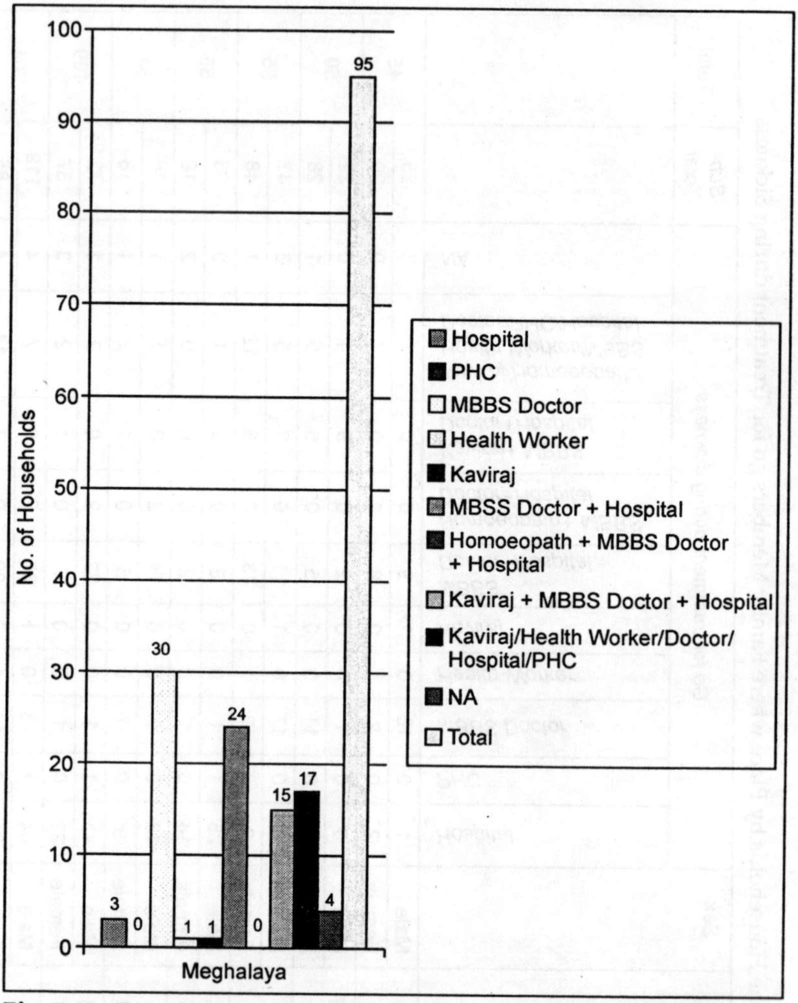

Fig. 7.60: Distribution of the Household Heads in Meghalaya by the Place where the Family Members go for Treatment during Sickness

We see that while only 3 of the total 95 household heads in Meghalaya confirmed that they went to the hospital for the treatment of their physical ailments, 66 out of the total 109 household heads in Tripura said that during their sickness, or even when their family members were ill, they used to visit the hospital for getting treatment. The existing gap in the distribution of household heads in the two States, so far as their visit to the hospital for treatment is concerned, indicates the non-existence of any reliable, adequately developed hospital infrastructure in the neighbourhood of the villages in Meghalaya.

It is surprising and at the same time unfortunate that none of the household heads in Ringkseh and Kyton-u-Mon in Meghalaya ever go to any primary health centre (PHC), indicating that there are no such centres in the village or at a close distance. However, only 1 female household head in Ringkseh has access to the health worker. The existence of PHCs in Tripura could also be considered a remote possibility as only 1 male head in Beltali confirmed that he visited such a treatment centre when any family member, including himself, was sick and had to be provided remedies.

25.26 per cent of the household heads in Meghalaya and 26.60 per cent of them in Tripura said that they visited the MBBS doctor and the hospital as well during any illness in the family. Except 2 male heads in Kalitila, Tripura none of the others consulted a homoeopath doctor and an MBBS doctor while going to the hospital at a time. Only 1 male head from Ringkseh, Meghalaya said that he consulted a Kaviraj during any illness in the family.

From the above trends we can assume that while the homoeopathic and ayurvedic treatment procedures were still not quite popular with the people, the practice of visiting quacks was also considered to be a backdated mode of treatment and was on the wane, at least in these villages of the two States. Nonetheless, we can also presume this to be the general trend in the States. Also, we have ample proofs about the need to develop the existing hospital infrastructure in both the States (Figs. 7.60 and 7.61).

Whether Immunization has been given to the Last Child

During data collection on the people's preferences and access to the different types of medication available to them during illnesses, the sample population has also been interviewed to find out whether or not the last child in the family has been immunized. The research team went about with this activity because they wanted to form an idea about the awareness of the people about the various child health development schemes of the government.

From Table 7.34 it is evident that a maximum proportion of the household heads (34.31%), both males and females, in

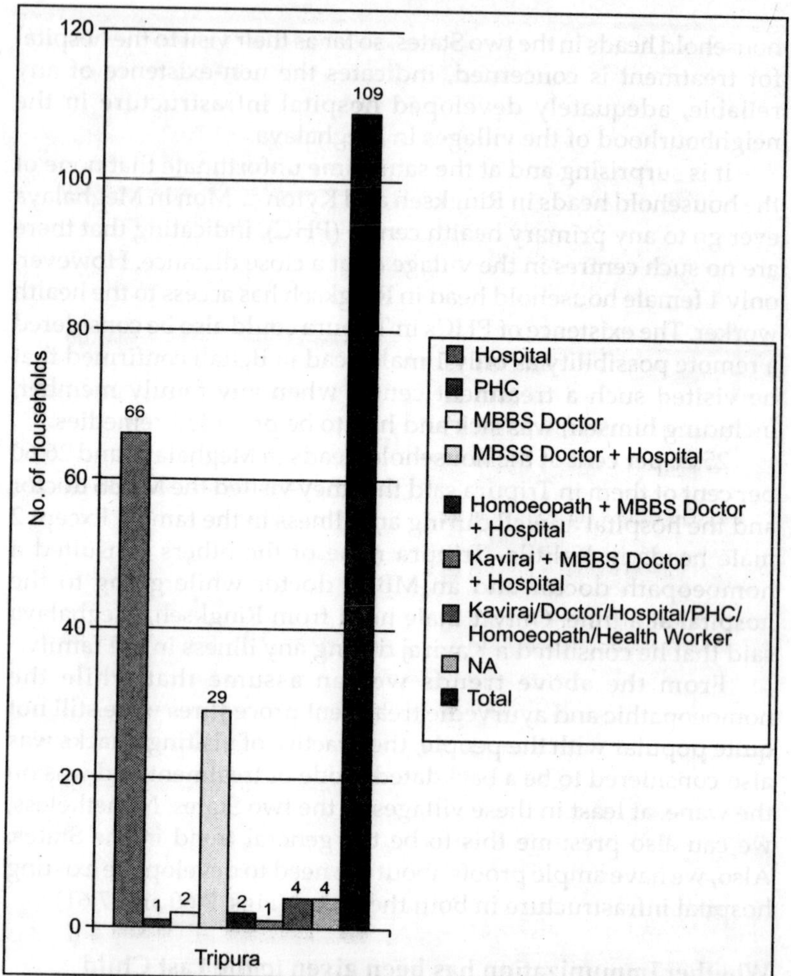

Fig. 7.61: Distribution of the Household Heads in Tripura by the Place where the Family Members go for Treatment during Sickness

Meghalaya and Tripura, immunized the last child in the family with vaccinations for BCG, triple antigen, polio and measles. The consciousness in respect of immunization was, however, more conspicuous among the people of Meghalaya, 43.15 per cent of whom confirmed in this regard as against a mere 26.60 per cent in Tripura.

Table 7.34: Distribution of the Households by Immunization of the Last Child

State	*Village*	*Sex*	*Immunization given*											
			BCG	*Tripleantigen*	*Polio*	*Measles*	*BCG and Tripleantigen*	*BCG and Polio*	*BCG, Tripleantigen and Polio*	*BCG, Tripleantigen, Polio and Measles*	*Others*	*NA*	*Sub Total*	*Total*
Meghalaya	Ringkseh	Male	3	0	0	0	0	0	1	16	0	5	25	45
		Female	4	0	0	0	0	1	0	13	0	2	20	
	Kyton-u-Mon	Male	1	0	0	0	0	4	5	6	0	6	22	50
		Female	2	0	0	0	0	7	0	6	2	11	28	
	Total	Male	4	0	0	0	0	4	6	22	0	11	47	95
		Female	6	0	0	0	0	8	0	19	2	13	48	
Tripura	Beltali	Male	0	0	2	0	1	9	0	12	3	9	36	55
		Female	0	0	3	0	0	2	0	3	0	11	19	
	Kalitila	Male	0	0	0	0	3	4	1	11	1	16	36	54
		Female	0	0	0	0	0	1	1	3	5	8	18	
	Total	Male	0	0	2	0	4	13	1	23	4	25	72	109
		Female	0	0	3	0	0	3	1	6	5	19	37	
Grand Total		Male	4	0	2	0	4	17	7	45	4	36	119	204
		Female	6	0	3	0	0	11	1	25	7	32	85	

That none of the people in either of the States were so much worried about the infection from measles is clear from the fact that none of them immunized their last child against measles exclusively. Rather, there were many people who chose to immunize their last child with BCG and triple antigen vaccination and polio drops, and ignored completely the need for the vaccination for measles. From this we could assume that the awareness of the people about the ill effects of measles is not yet adequate.

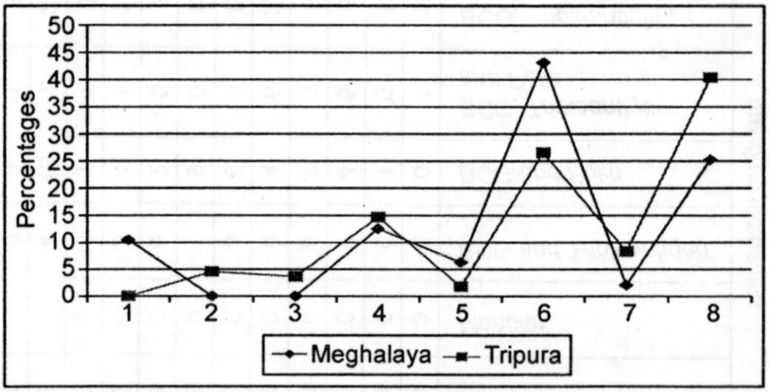

1 — BCG, 2 — Polio, 3 — BCG and Tripleantigen, 4 — BCG and Polio , 5 — BCG, Tripleantigen and Polio, 6 — BCG, Tripleantigen, Polio and Measles, 7 — Others, 8 — NA

Fig. 7.62: Distribution of the Household Heads by Immunization of Last Child

The indications are that there should be awareness generation programmes in all the villages in this respect, if we are truly keen to see the well-being of the beneficiary children through the success of the immunization programme (Fig. 7.62).

Time of Food Intake

In India it is the custom in many families to serve a meal first to the male members in the family. The female members generally ate after them. But considering the changing family and social situations and the associated conveniences that go along, this trend is also changing to a large extent. We have collected relevant data to decipher the prevailing trends in this respect in the female-headed households in the two north-eastern States included in the study, which have found inclusion in Table 7.35.

Table 7.35: Distribution of the Female-Headed Households by Time of Food Intake

State	*Village*	*Take Food*				*Total*
		All together	*After males have their meals*	*Whenever needed/when it is convenient*	*Any Other*	
Meghalaya	Ringkseh	0	0	20 (100)	0	20 (41.67)
	Kyton-u-Mon	2 (7.14)	0	26 (92.86)	0	28 (58.33)
	Total	2 (4.17)	0	46 (95.83)	0	48 (56.47)
Tripura	Beltali	14 (73.68)	4 (21.05)	1 (5.27)	0	19 (51.35)
	Kalitila	11 (61.11)	2 (11.11)	5 (27.78)	0	18 (48.65)
	Total	25 (67.57)	6 (16.22)	6 (16.22)	0	37 (43.53)
Grand Total		27 (31.76)	6 (7.06)	52 (61.18)	0	85 (100)

Table 7.35 reveals that 25 out of the 37 female-headed households (67.56%) in Tripura have all the family members sitting together for their meals. Contrastingly, this trend prevails in only 2 out of the 48 female-headed households (4.16%) in Meghalaya.

Again, although the custom of the female members taking their meals after the male members is totally absent in Meghalaya, 16.21 per cent of the female-headed households in Tripura conform to this tradition even now.

Interestingly, in a maximum number of the female-headed households (95.83%) in Meghalaya, the members adjust their time of food intake according to their convenience.

Thus from the above we see that although it is still considered a custom in many families in India for the females to take their meals after the males are done with it, it is not so conspicuous in the north-eastern States. In Meghalaya in particular, this custom does not exist at all (Fig. 7.63).

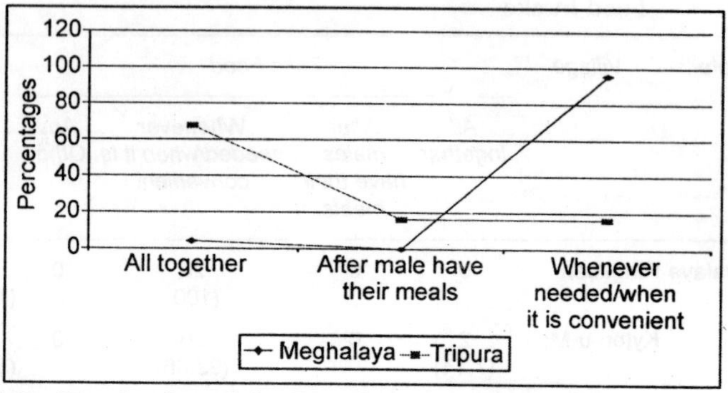

Fig. 7.63: Distribution of the Female-Headed Households by the Time of Food Intake

(F) PSYCHOLOGICAL EMPOWERMENT

By assessing if or not the women in the places under survey are empowered psychologically, we aim at determining whether or not they have satisfaction about their status as individuals alongside their male counterparts—if they like to enjoy some autonomy, or they prefer partial subjugation or complete dependence on the males.

On Dependency on Men

The data on the views of the male and female household heads on the dependency of women on men are given in Table 7.36(a) while Table 7.36(b) gives us details of the data collected in this regard from the counterparts of the household heads.

An analytical study of Table 7.36(a) reveals that in Meghalaya, most of the female heads (68.75%) did not think in terms of their dependency on men. However, 16.67 per cent of them have admitted that they thought about dependency on men while 14.58 per cent admitted that they were not sure of how to consider this aspect. It is also clear that about 79 per cent of the female household heads from Ringkseh and Kyton-u-Mon villages in Meghalaya do

Table 7.36(a): Distribution by Thinking of the Head of the Households about the Dependency (Economic and Non-Economic) on Men

State	*Village*	*Sex*	*Thinking about Dependency on Men*			*Wants Women to be Dependent on Men*			*Sub Total*	*Total*
			Yes	*No*	*Not Sure*	*Yes*	*No*	*Not Sure*		
Meghalaya	Ringkseh	Male	4 (16)	15 (60)	6 (24)	3 (12)	17 (68)	5 (20)	25 (55.56)	45 (47.37)
		Female	3 (15)	13 (65)	4 (20)	3 (15)	13 (65)	4 (20)	20 (44.44)	
	Kyton-u-Mon	Male	6 (27.27)	12 (54.55)	4 (18.18)	4 (18.18)	16 (72.73)	2 (9.09)	22 (44)	50 (52.63)
		Female	5 (17.86)	20 (71.43)	3 (10.71)	2 (7.14)	25 (89.29)	1 (3.57)	28 (56)	
	Total	Male	10 (21.28)	27 (57.45)	10 (21.28)	7 (14.89)	33 (70.21)	7 (14.89)	47 (49.97)	95 (46.57)
		Female	8 (16.67)	33 (68.75)	7 (14.58)	5 (10.42)	38 (79.17)	5 (10.42)	48 (50.53)	
Tripura	Beltali	Male	33 (91.67)	2 (5.56)	1 (2.78)	10 (27.78)	24 (66.67)	2 (5.56)	36 (65.45)	55 (50.46)
		Female	9 (47.37)	10 (52.63)	0	10 (52.63)	9 (47.37)	0	19 (34.55)	
	Kalitila	Male	36 (100)	0	0	12 (33.33)	24 (66.67)	0	36 (66.67)	54 (49.54)
		Female	8 (44.44)	9 (50)	1 (5.56)	5 (27.78)	11 (61.11)	2 (11.11)	18 (33.33)	
	Total	Male	69 (95.83)	2 (2.78)	1 (1.39)	22 (30.56)	48 (66.67)	2 (2.78)	72 (66.06)	109 (53.43)
		Female	17 (45.95)	19 (51.35)	1 (2.70)	15 (40.54)	20 (54.05)	2 (5.41)	37 (33.94)	
Grand Total		Male	79 (66.37)	29 (24.37)	11 (9.24)	29 (24.37)	81 (68.07)	9 (7.56)	119 (58.33)	204 (100)
		Female	25 (29.41)	52 (61.18)	8 (9.41)	20 (23.53)	58 (68.24)	7 (8.24)	85 (41.67)	
		Total	104 (50.98)	81 (39.71)	19 (9.31)	49 (24.02)	149 (73.04)	16 (7.84)	204 (100)	

Table 7.36(b): Distribution of the Counterparts of the Household Heads by their Way of Thinking about the Dependency (Economic and Non-Economic) on Men

State	Village	Sex	Thinking about Dependency on Men			Wants Women to be Dependent on Men			Sub Total	Total
			Yes	No	Not Sure	Yes	No	Not Sure		
Meghalaya	Ringkseh	Male	3	10	3	1	14	1	16	35
		Female	3	13	3	0	16	3	19	
	Kyton-u-Mon	Male	2	17	1	1	18	1	20	41
		Female	6	14	1	5	15	1	21	
	Total	Male	5	27	4	2	32	2	36	76
		Female	9	27	4	5	31	4	40	
Tripura	Beltali	Male	8	9	0	2	15	0	17	53
		Female	33	2	1	21	13	2	36	
	Kalitila	Male	8	6	0	3	11	0	14	50
		Female	36	0	0	23	13	0	36	
	Total	Male	16	15	0	5	26	0	31	103
		Female	69	2	1	44	26	2	72	
Grand Total		Male	21	42	4	7	58	2	67	
		Female	78	29	5	49	57	6	112	179
		Total	99	71	9	56	115	8	179	

not want women to be dependent on men, while 10.42 per cent of them spoke in favour of dependence of women on men.

In Tripura also, 10 out of the 19 female heads in Beltali and 9 out of the 18 female heads from Kalitila, accounting for 51.35 per cent of the total number of female household heads included under the purview of this research study in the State, have firmly stated that they did not think in terms of their dependency on men. The distribution of the sample female heads in the two villages who wanted women in general not to be dependent on men was 54.05 per cent

Let us consider next the views as confided by the male household heads in the concerned villages. Table 7.36(a) indicates that overall, while majority (57.45%) of the male household heads in Meghalaya opined that women need not be dependent on menfolk, the situation in Tripura is just the reverse with the balance tilted in favour of 95.83 per cent male heads who opined that they supported the dependence of women on them.

Table 7.36(b) shows the distribution of the counterparts of the household heads by their way of thinking about the economic and non-economic dependence of women on men.

But if we consider the counterparts of the household heads, then it will be noticed that in Tripura almost 96 per cent of the female counterparts strongly support their dependency on men. Again, 61.11 per cent of them ruled in favour of women's dependence on men.

In this context it is interesting to note that 48.38 per cent of the male counterparts did not think about women's dependency on men and 83.87 per cent of them did not want women to depend on men for economic and non-economic reasons.

Training Programme towards Self-Sufficiency

In order to find out about the perception of the male and female household heads on whether the participation of women in training programmes would really ensure that they attained self-sufficiency, the researchers asked each and every one of them about their opinion. The answers given by the sample population has found representation in Table 7.37(a) below.

From Table 7.37(a) it is clear that maximum number of the household heads from both the States, (percentage-wise 87.25)

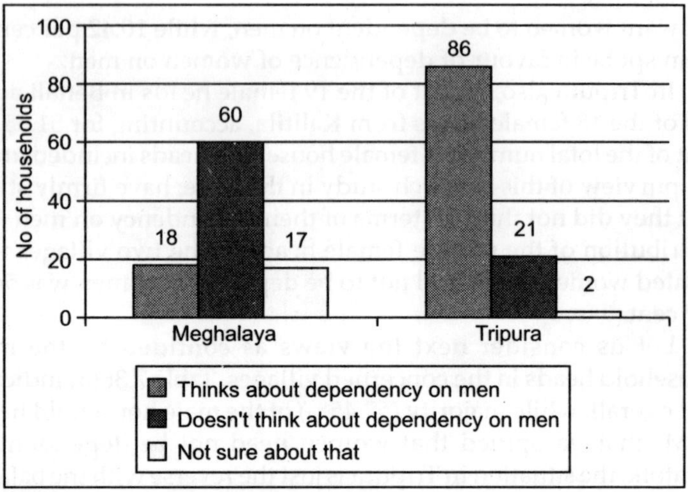

Fig. 7.64: Distribution of the Household Heads by their Way of Thinking about the Dependency on Men

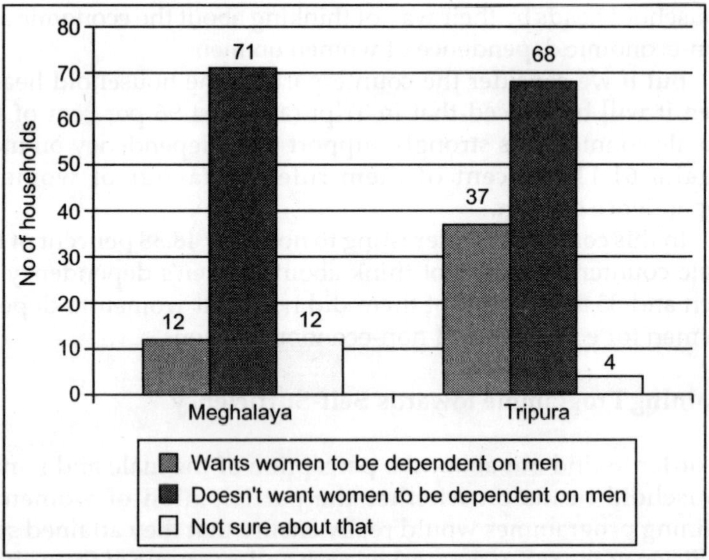

Fig. 7.65: Distribution of the Household Heads by their Opinion about Women's Dependence on Men

Table 7.37(a): Distribution of the Households by the Perception of the Household Heads on Whether Training Programme for Women is towards Self-Sufficiency

State	*Village*	*Sex*	*Training Programme towards self-sufficiency*				*Sub Total*	*Total*
			Yes	*No*	*Not Sure*	*No Idea*		
Meghalaya	Ringkseh	Male	24	0	0	1	25	45
		Female	17	0	0	3	20	
	Kyton-u-Mon	Male	19	0	0	3	22	50
		Female	22	0	0	6	28	
	Total	Male	43	0	0	4	47	95
		Female	39	0	0	9	48	
Tripura	Beltali	Male	31	2	1	2	36	55
		Female	14	1	2	2	19	
	Kalitila	Male	35	1	0	0	36	54
		Female	16	0	2	0	18	
	Total	Male	66	3	1	2	72	109
		Female	30	1	4	2	37	
Grand Total		Male	109	3	1	6	119	204
		Female	69	1	4	11	85	
		Total	178	4	5	17	204	

validated that women should be allowed to participate in training programmes for self-sufficiency. Gender-wise, in both the States together, 109 out of the total 119 male household heads and 69 out of 85 female heads agreed that the training programmes for women would take them towards their self-sufficiency.

As Table 7.37(b) confirms, 87.5 per cent of the female counterparts of the household heads and 86.56 per cent of the male counterparts also confirm their belief that the training programmes for women would help them achieve self-sufficiency (Fig. 7.66).

On Women Visiting the Nearest Town

How much liberty did the women folk in the sample villages have so far as going out of their homes to places outside the periphery of their homes is concerned? Women of which age group frequented out to the nearest town, alone? What was the distribution of the women who went to the nearest town escorted

Table 7.37(b): Distribution of the Households by the Perception of the Counterparts of the Household Heads on Whether Training Programme for Women is Towards Self-Sufficiency

State	Village	Sex	Training Programme towards self-sufficiency				Sub Total	Total
			Yes	No	Not Sure	No Idea		
Megha aya	Ringkseh	Male	13	1	0	2	16	35
		Female	19	0	0	0	19	
	Kyton-u-Mon	Male	14	2	0	4	20	41
		Female	19	0	0	2	21	
	Total	Male	27	3	0	6	36	76
		Female	38	0	0	2	40	
Tripura	Beltali	Male	17	0	0	0	17	53
		Female	27	4	4	1	36	
	Kalitila	Male	14	0	0	0	14	50
		Female	33	0	2	1	36	
	Total	Male	31	0	0	0	31	103
		Female	60	4	6	2	72	
Grand Total		Male	58	3	0	6	67	179
		Female	98	4	6	4	112	
		Total	156	7	6	10	179	

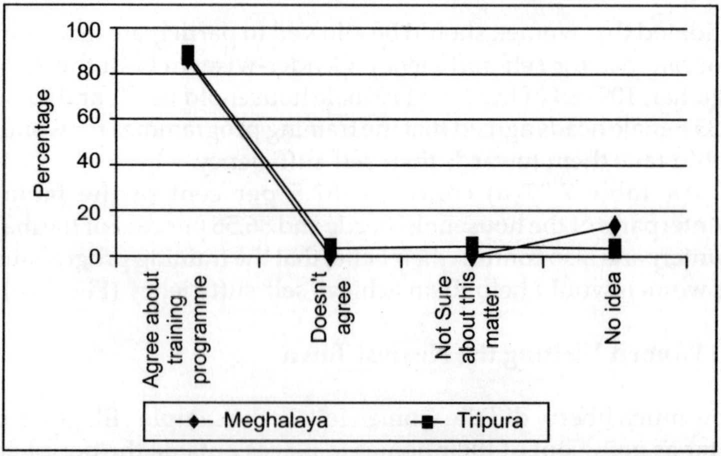

Fig. 7.66: Distribution of the Household Heads by the Perception on whether Training Programme for Women is Towards Self-Sufficiency

by their family members? Table 7.38 below highlights the empowerment of women in the context of all these aspects through the answers provided by the interviewed female heads.

As per the data in Table 7.38, the women from Meghalaya were more advanced in their outlook so far as visiting the nearest town without the permission of male members is concerned. This fact emerges from the fact that 89.58 per cent of Meghalaya's women visited the nearest town alone, without being escorted by their husbands or any other family member. A maximum out of them were in the age-group of 41-60, closely followed by the women above 60 years of age. Only 10.42 per cent of them moved out of their villages escorted by family members and others.

Comparatively, only 45.94 per cent of the women in Tripura visited the nearest town alone and unescorted. The remaining 54.06 per cent of the women needed someone or the other, either from their family or from some other family known to them (Fig. 7.67).

Freedom to Move Out of the Village

In the previous discussion, we made an attempt to unravel the empowerment of women in the context of their liberty to visit the nearest town alone. Closely related to that is this one that is an attempt at finding out about the freedom that the women in the sample villages were given by their family members to move outside their villages of residence.

According to Table 7.39(a), in Meghalaya State, irrespective of their literacy status, all the female household heads have the freedom to move outside their village. But in Tripura State, only 11 out of 37 female household heads have some freedom to move outside the village. At least 19 female household heads, or more than half the female household heads who have been included in this survey, have no freedom to move outside the village.

The above observations indicate the fact that women in Meghalaya have a better social and familial footing than the women in Tripura. It is surprising that 81.81 per cent of the women in Tripura who have the freedom to move outside the village are illiterate, implying that the literate female heads in the State's villages are still quite conservative in their approach and attitude.

Again, although the situations in Meghalaya and Tripura are contrasting, yet the fact that 30 out of the 48 female heads from

Table 7.38: Distribution of the Female Household Heads by their Visit to the Nearest Town without the Permission of Male Members

State	Village	Age Group	Visit to nearest town			Total
			Alone	With men or women from the same or other family	Others	
Meghalaya	Ringkseh	20-40	4	0	0	20
		41-60	8	0	0	
		> 60	7	1	0	
	Kyton-u-Mon	20-40	6	0	2	28
		41-60	9	2	0	
		> 60	9	0	0	
	Total	20-40	10	0	2	48
		41-60	17	2	0	
		> 60	16	1	0	
Tripura	Beltali	20-40	0	0	0	19
		41-60	2	0	7	
		> 60	3	0	7	
	Kalitila	20-40	3	0	0	18
		41-60	6	0	1	
		> 60	3	1	4	
	Total	20-40	3	0	0	37
		41-60	8	0	8	
		> 60	6	1	11	
Grand Total		20-40	13	0	2	85
		41-60	25	2	8	
		> 60	22	2	11	

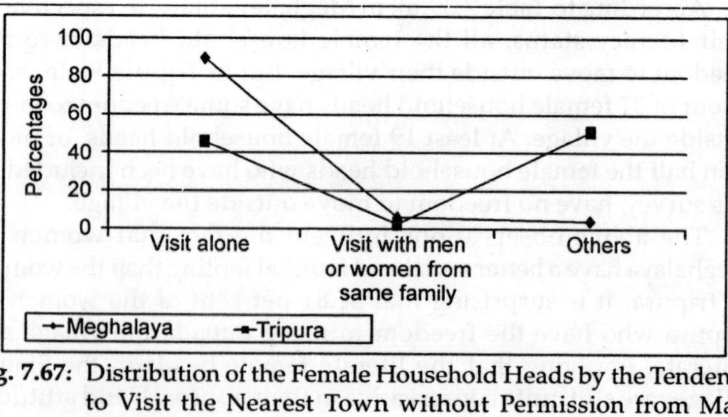

Fig. 7.67: Distribution of the Female Household Heads by the Tendency to Visit the Nearest Town without Permission from Male Members

Meghalaya, who had the freedom to move outside their village of residence, were literate is an indicator of the fact that literacy status is a major factor for these social changes.

Moreover, with the trend of moving outside the village for work or other reasons has caught up with the illiterate women in Tripura as well, the obvious implication is that irrespective of literacy status, there is a rise in women's consciousness about her rights and responsibilities. Besides, the family too is generally supportive to her in respect of enabling her to carry on social, economical, culture and political activities uninterruptedly (Fig. 7.68).

An attempt has been made to review the situation of women in details in so far as their freedom to move to places outside the village, unescorted by the male members of the family, is concerned and the relevant data collected is reproduced in Table 7.39(b).

The common places outside the village that were frequented by the women in Meghalaya are the marketplace, cinema hall, video parlour, temple or church, school or college and other public places. Like for instance, except 1, all the other female heads in the villages of Meghalaya went to the market as and when required, without their male counterparts. The other places frequented regularly by the women in Meghalaya were the places of worship and relatives' houses.

In Tripura, there were lesser number of women who went to the above-mentioned places outside the villages unescorted.

Equal Pay for Men and Women for the Same Work

The household heads, both males and females, have also been interviewed with the intention of finding out about their viewpoints on payment of wages and salaries to women: whether or not it should be equal with that of the males. The details of the findings are shown in Table 7.40(a).

The interpretation of Table 7.40(a) is made hereafter. So far as equality in the distribution of wages and salaries to males and females is concerned, it is obvious that the male heads from Tripura were more liberal in their viewpoint; this is evident from our finding that 75 per cent of the total male heads in the State have expressed in favour of equal pay for men and women engaged in similar kinds of work. On the other hand, only 25.53 per cent of

Table 7.39(a): Distribution of the Female Household Heads by their Freedom to Move Outside the Village

State	*Village*	*Literacy Status*	*Freedom to move outside village*			*Total*
			Have Freedom	Haven't Freedom	No Comments	
Meghalaya	Ringkseh	Illiterate	2	0	0	20
		<Madhyamik	15	0	0	
		>Madhyamik	3	0	0	
	Sub Total		20	0	0	28
	Kyton-u-Mon	Illiterate	16	0	0	
		<Madhyamik	8	0	0	
		>Madhyamik	4	0	0	48
	Sub Total		28	0	0	
	Total		48	0	0	
Tripura	Beltali	Illiterate	5	6	2	19
		<Madhyamik	1	2	3	
		>Madhyamik	0	0	0	
	Sub Total		6	8	5	18
	Kalitila	Illiterate	4	4	1	
		<Madhyamik	1	7	1	
		>Madhyamik	0	0	0	37
	Subtotal		5	11	2	
	Total		11	19	7	
Grand Total			59	19	7	85

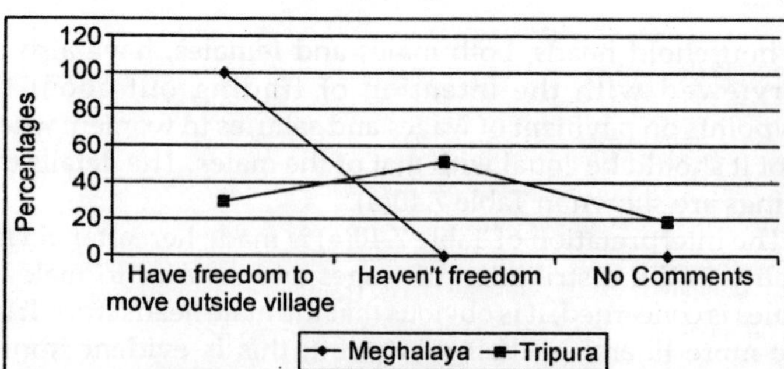

Fig. 7.68: Distribution of the Female Household Heads by their Freedom to Move Outside the Village

Table 7.39(b): Distribution of the Female Household Heads by their Freedom to Move Outside the Village without the Male Members of their Family

State	Village	Literacy Status	Move outside village without male members																		Total
			Market			Cinema/ Video			Mandir/ Church			Relatives' House			School/ College			Other Public Place			
			Yes	No	No Comments	Yes	No	No Comments	Yes	No	No Comments	Yes	No	No Comments	Yes	No	No Comments	Yes	No	No Comments	
Meghalaya	Ring-kseh	Illiterate	2	0	0	2	0	0	2	0	0	2	0	0	2	0	0	2	0	0	20
		<Madhyamik	15	0	0	11	0	4	15	0	0	15	0	0	13	0	2	15	0	0	
		>Madhyamik	3	0	0	3	0	0	3	0	0	3	0	0	3	0	0	3	0	0	
	Kyton-u-Mon	Illiterate	15	0	1	2	8	6	14	0	2	15	0	1	11	0	5	15	0	1	28
		<Madhyamik	8	0	0	2	4	2	7	0	1	8	0	0	6	0	2	8	0	0	
		>Madhyamik	4	0	0	1	2	1	4	0	0	4	0	0	2	0	2	4	0	0	
Tripura	Beltali	Illiterate	3	0	10	1	0	12	2	0	11	2	0	11	0	0	13	4	0	9	19
		<Madhyamik	1	0	5	0	0	6	0	0	6	1	0	5	0	0	6	1	0	5	
		>Madhyamik	0	0	0	0	0	0	0	0	0	0	0	0	0	0	0	0	0	0	
	Kalitila	Illiterate	2	1	6	0	1	8	2	1	6	2	1	6	0	1	8	2	1	6	18
		<Madhyamik	5	0	4	1	0	8	4	0	5	5	0	4	3	0	6	2	0	7	
		>Madhyamik	0	0	0	0	0	0	0	0	0	0	0	0	0	0	0	0	0	0	
Grand Total			58	1	26	23	15	47	53	1	31	57	1	27	40	1	44	56	1	28	85

the male heads in Meghalaya think that there should be equal pay for men and women for the same work.

Among the female heads too, the females of Tripura (72.97%) were more in favour of equal pay for men and women.

All these are indicative of the fact that the economic condition of the people of Meghalaya is better off than those of Tripura, and hence the need for money among the sample population in Tripura is more acute (Fig. 7.69).

Table 7.40(b), which reveals the distribution of the counterparts of the household heads in their views on equal pay for men and women for the same work, shows that a major portion of the male (75%) and female (72.5%) counterparts in Meghalaya do not think in terms of equal pay from men and women. In Tripura, on the other hand, 83.9 per cent of the male and 72.2 per cent of the female counterparts have ruled in favour of equal pay for men and women.

Rights to Inherit Property

With the initiatives taken by the Government of India, today women too are equal in status with men in matters of inheritance of property. Are the changes in this respect palpable in the States included under the purview of this research study? What are the views of the household heads regarding inheritance of property? A glimpse at Table 7.41(a) will give the answers to our query.

From Table 7.41(a) we can conclude that most of the male (97.87%) and female (93.75%) household heads in Meghalaya opined that children should have inheritance rights, irrespective of their sex. While only 1 male head in the State is unsure of his stand in this regard, 3 female heads either refused to make any comment on this or have told that they were unsure of taking a resolute stand on this issue.

The household heads in Tripura who agreed in favour of equal rights for male and female children to inherit property are in a majority, with 77.77 per cent males and 64.9 per cent of the female household heads belonging to this category.

Combining the strength of the household heads in both the States, it is noticed that 102 out of the total 119 male household heads and 69 out of the 85 female household heads consider that male and female children should have equal rights of inheritance.

Table 7.40(a): Distribution of the Household Heads based on the Opinion in Favour of Equal Pay for Men and Women for the Same Work

State	Village	Sex	Age Group	Thinks about Equal Pay			Sub Total	Total
				Agree	Not Agree	Not Sure		
Meghalaya	Ringkseh	Male	20-40	1	7	0	25 (55.56)	45 (47.37)
			41-60	1	6	1		
			>60	2	7	0		
		Female	20-40	3	1	0	20 (44.44)	
			41-60	2	6	0		
			>60	0	8	0		
	Kyton-u-Mon	Male	20-40	3	4	1	22 (44)	50 (52.63)
			41-60	3	7	0		
			>60	2	2	0		
		Female	20-40	4	4	0	28 (56)	
			41-60	5	6	0		
			>60	3	4	2		
	Total	Male		12(25.53)	33(70.21)	2(4.26)	47(49.47)	95 (46.57)
		Female		17(35.42)	29(60.42)	2(4.17)	48(50.53)	
Tripura	Beltali	Male	20-40	11	1	0	36 (65.45)	55 (50.46)
			41-60	9	6	1		
			>60	3	5	0		
		Female	20-40	0	0	0	19 (34.55)	
			41-60	7	2	1		
			>60	7	0	2		
	Kalitila	Male	20-40	18	0	0	36 (66.67)	54 (49.54)
			41-60	11	3	1		
			>60	2	1	0		
		Female	20-40	2	1	0	18 (33.33)	
			41-60	5	2	0		
			>60	6	1	1		
	Total	Male		54 (75)	16 (22.22)	2 (2.78)	72 (66.06)	109 (53.43)
		Female		27 (72.97)	6 (16.22)	4 (10.81)	37 (33.94)	
Grand Total		Male		66 (55.46)	49 (41.18)	4 (3.36)	119 (58.33)	204 (100)
		Female		44 (51.76)	35 (41.18)	6 (7.06)	85 (41.67)	
		Total		110 (53.92)	84 (41.18)	10 (4.90)	204 (100)	

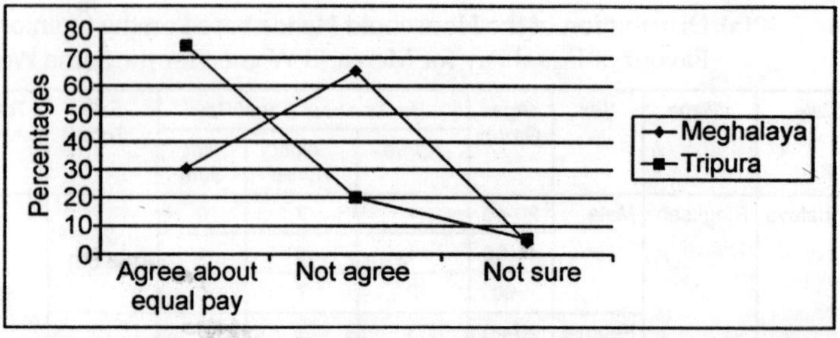

Fig. 7.69: Distribution of the Household Heads based on the Opinion on Equal Pay for Men and Women for the Same Work

Table 7.40(b): Distribution of the Counterparts of the Household Heads Based on the Opinion in Favour of Equal Pay for Men and Women for the Same Work

State	*Village*	*Sex*	*Thinks about Equal Pay*			*Sub Total*	*Total*
			Agree	*Not Agree*	*Not Sure*		
Meghalaya	Ringkseh	Male	3	13	0	16	35
		Female	1	18	0	19	
	Kyton-u-Mon	Male	4	14	2	20	41
		Female	8	11	2	21	
	Total	Male	7(19.4)	27(75)	2(5.6)	36	76
		Female	9(22.5)	29(72.5)	2(5)	40	
Tripura	Beltali	Male	13	4	0	17	53
		Female	25	6	5	36	
	Kalitila	Male	13	1	0	14	50
		Female	27	5	4	36	
	Total	Male	26(83.9)	5(16.1)	0	31	103
		Female	52(72.2)	11(15.3)	9(12.5)	72	
Grand Total		Male	33	32	2	67	179
		Female	61	40	11	112	

There are about 20 household heads out of the total 204 household heads who do not agree with the above feature (Fig. 7.70).

The counterparts of the household heads were also asked separately for their views on the rights of children to inherit property—whether or not they consider there should be equal distribution of status between the male and female children in this regard.

Table 7.41(a): Distribution of the Household Heads on the basis of their View that All Children should have Equal Rights to Inherit Property

State	Village	Sex	Thinking that all the children have equal rights to inherit property				Sub Total	Total
			Agree	Not agree	Not sure	No comments		
Meghalaya	Ringkseh	Male	25	0	0	0	25	45
		Female	20	0	0	0	20	
	Kyton-u-Mon	Male	21	0	1	0	22	50
		Female	25	0	1	2	28	
	Total	Male	46	0	1	0	47	95
		Female	45	0	1	2	48	
Tripura	Beltali	Male	24	9	1	2	36	55
		Female	11	3	2	3	19	
	Kalitila	Male	32	4	0	0	36	54
		Female	13	4	1	0	18	
	Total	Male	56	13	1	2	72	109
		Female	24	7	3	3	37	
Grand Total		Male	102	13	2	2	119	204
		Female	69	7	4	5	85	

Table 7.41(b) which shows the outcome of our findings indicates that the result for the counterparts of the household heads is more or less the same as that of the household heads themselves, whether in Meghalaya or in Tripura.

Reservation of Seats for Women as Members in the Gram Panchayat

The parties in power in the different States of the country and the opposition parties as well have unanimously passed the ruling to the effect that there should be 33 per cent reservation of seats for women in the political process at the national level, State level, district level and village level too. So the research team interviewed the household heads in an attempt to find out how well this ruling was received by the people in the sample villages in the States of Meghalaya and Tripura regarding reservation of seats for women as members in the Gram Panchayat. The findings have been shown in Table 7.42(a) hereafter.

Fig. 7.70: Distribution of the Household Heads based on the Judgement that all Children should have Equal Rights to Inherit Property

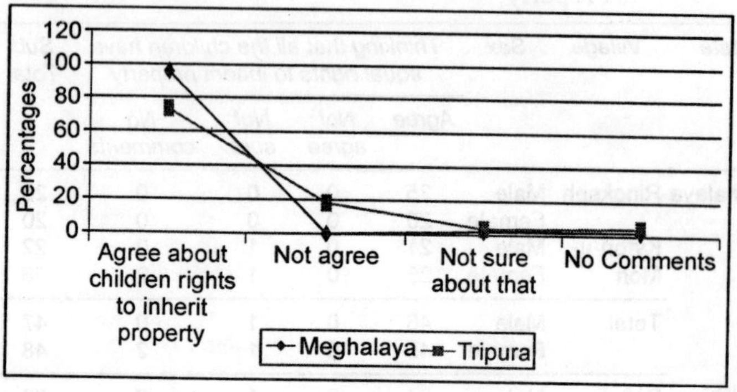

Table 7.41(b): Distribution of the Counterparts of the Household Heads on the basis of their View that All Children should have Equal Rights to Inherit Property

State	*Village*	*Sex*	*Thinking that all the children have equal rights to inherit property*				*Sub Total*	*Total*
			Agree	*Not agree*	*Not sure*	*No comments*		
Meghalaya	Ringkseh	Male	14	0	2	0	16	35
		Female	17	1	1	0	19	
	Kyton-u-Mon	Male	16	0	2	2	20	41
		Female	20	1	0	0	21	
	Total	Male	30	0	4	2	36	76
		Female	37	2	1	0	40	
Tripura	Beltali	Male	15	1	1	0	17	53
		Female	23	11	2	0	36	
	Kalitila	Male	13	1	0	0	14	50
		Female	26	9	1	0	36	
	Total	Male	28	2	1	0	31	103
		Female	49	20	3	0	72	
Grand Total		Male	58	2	5	2	67	179
		Female	86	22	4	0	112	

The response from the household heads on the reservation of seats for women in the Gram Panchayat, as revealed in Table 7.42(a), did not yield quite similar results in the two States.

It is surprising that a significant proportion of the female heads in Meghalaya, along with the male heads, vehemently opposed the concept of women actively participating in the political process as elected members in the Gram Panchayat. The percentage distributions of the male and female heads in the State who are opposed to reservation of seats for women in the Gram Panchayat are 76.6 and 79.16 respectively. The number of household heads who opined in favour of seat reservation for women in the Gram Panchayat is negligible in the State.

Contrastingly, although in many other aspects discussed earlier, we have evidences of the rejection of a traditional outlook among the household heads in Meghalaya as compared to the household heads in Tripura, in matters related to seat reservation in the Gram Panchayat for women, the household heads in Tripura are more modern in their views.

In fact none of the male and female household heads in the two villages oppose the government's stand in respect of seat reservation in the Gram Panchayat for women. 62 out of 72 male heads (86.11%) and 28 out of 37 female heads (75.67%) have welcomed the ruling on reservation of seats in the Gram Panchayat for women. Not a single household head in the State has opposed the ruling directing reservation of seats in the political process for women. Of course there is a handful of household heads who are a bit hesitant to give their decision, however, they too have opined that seat reservation for women is not so bad after that (Fig. 7.71).

As Table 7.42(b) unfolds that the opinion of the counterparts of the household heads about the reservation of seats for women members in the Gram Panchayat is almost the same in Meghalaya and Tripura also.

Opinion about where the Last Baby was Born

Not very long ago, the practice in most Indian villages so far as giving birth to children was concerned was to make full-fledged arrangements for handling delivery cases at the pregnant woman's home only. However, with the improvement in the health infrastructure and the establishment of hospitals and primary health centres in the rural areas as well, as also because of the growing awareness among the rural people about the benefits of treatment for their ailments in the hospitals and health centres, a

Table 7.42(a): Distribution of the Household Heads by their Opinion about the Reservation of Seats for Women in the Gram Panchayat

State	Village	Sex	Opinion						Sub Total	Total
			Very bad	Bad	Not so bad	Good	Very Good	No Idea		
Meghalaya	Ringkseh	Male	20	0	5	0	0	0	25	45
		Female	19	0	0	1	0	0	20	
	Kyton-u-Mon	Male	12	4	0	1	0	5	22	50
		Female	10	9	1	0	0	8	28	
	Total	Male	32	4	5	1	0	5	47	95
		Female	29	9	1	1	0	8	48	
Tripura	Beltali	Male	0	0	4	14	18	0	36	55
		Female	0	0	6	9	4	0	19	
	Kalitila	Male	0	0	6	16	14	0	36	54
		Female	0	0	3	8	7	0	18	
	Total	Male	0	0	10	30	32	0	72	109
		Female	0	0	9	17	11	0	37	
Grand Total		Male	32	4	15	31	32	5	119	204
		Female	29	9	10	18	11	8	85	
		Total	61	13	25	49	43	13	204	

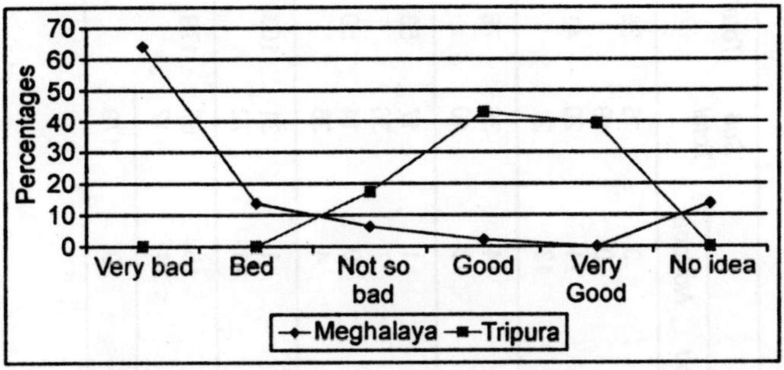

Fig. 7.71: Distribution of the Household Heads by their Opinion about the Reservation of Seats for Women in the Gran Panchayat

sizable number of them have been visiting these centres for consulting the doctors there about their health problems.

To get an idea about the local people's stances in the surveyed villages, they were asked to provide the data on where their last child in the family was born—in a hospital or at home, or elsewhere. The findings have been detailed in Table 7.43.

Table 7.43 shows the distribution of the household heads on the basis of their opinions about where the last baby was born. As is evident, in both the States, a maximum number of the respondents have informed that the last child in their family was born at home, or in other words, arrangements for delivery were made at home only. 62.10 per cent and 66.97 per cent of all the household heads interviewed in Meghalaya and Tripura respectively confided that the last child in their family was born at home.

From the above it could be surmised that the people are generally reluctant to break the family tradition of childbirth at home, unaware of the demerits of this practice. Again, another implication is that there were no dependable health centres or hospitals in the vicinity of the villages and those who could afford to travel the big distance to the nearest health centre could only avail of the scopes of hospital treatment.

However, the people were gradually getting accustomed to availing of the health infrastructure that exists for or near in the region. That is why as many as 29 out of 95 household heads from Ringkseh and Kyton-u-Mon in Meghalaya and 21 out of 109 household heads in Tripura confirmed that the last child in their respective families was born in a hospital (Fig. 7.72).

Table 7.42(b): Distribution of the Counterparts of the Household Heads by their Opinion about the Reservation of Seats for Women in the Gram Panchayat

State	Village	Sex	Opinion						Sub Total	Total
			Very bad	Bad	Not so bad	Good	Very Good	No Idea		
Meghalaya	Ringkseh	Male	4	1	6	1	1	3	16	35
		Female	9	0	10	0	0	0	19	
	Kyton-u-Mon	Male	4	3	0	2	0	11	20	41
		Female	3	4	0	1	0	13	21	
	Total	Male	8	4	6	3	1	14	36	76
		Female	12	4	10	1	0	13	40	
Tripura	Beltali	Male	0	0	1	8	7	1	17	53
		Female	0	0	4	20	5	7	36	
	Kalitila	Male	0	0	1	2	11	0	14	50
		Female	0	0	11	14	7	4	36	
	Total	Male	0	0	2	10	18	1	31	103
		Female	0	0	15	34	12	11	72	
Grand Total		Male	8	4	8	13	19	15	67	179
		Female	12	4	25	35	12	24	112	
		Total	20	8	33	48	31	39	179	

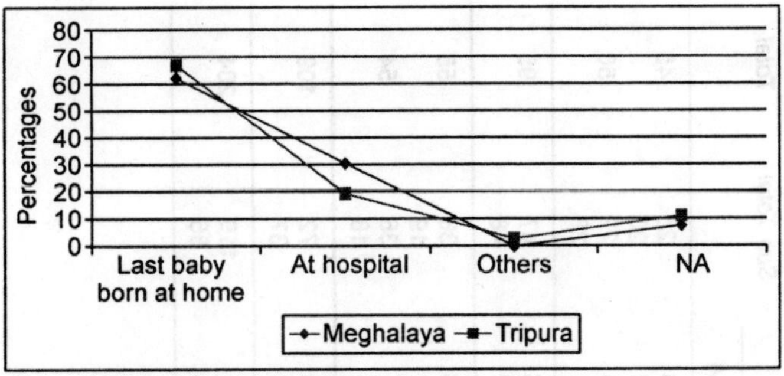

Note: NA = Not answered.

Fig. 7.72: Distribution of the Household Heads by their Opinion about where the Last Baby was born

Religious Empowerment

Visit Church/Temple

How much free were the women in the surveyed villages to visit their places of worship? Did they have the permission from the family members to visit these places regularly or were they guided by the dictates of their own religion? We can get a rough idea about all these queries from the data entered in Table 7.44(a).

According to Table 7.44(a), in Meghalaya, 31 male household heads and 31 female household heads out of the total of 47 male and 48 female household heads visited church/temple everyday or once a week. In this context it may be informed that a maximum

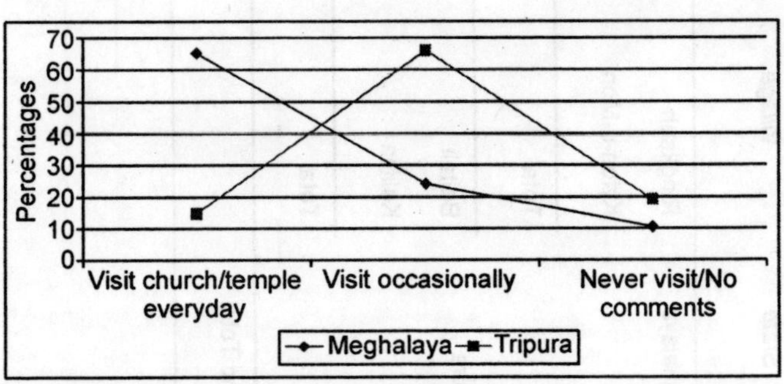

Fig. 7.73: Distribution of the Household Heads according to their Visit to Church/Temple

Table 7.43: Distribution of the Household Heads by their Opinion about where the Last Baby was Born

State	*Village*	*Sex*	*Where was the last baby born*				*Sub Total*	*Total*
			Home	*Hospital*	*Others*	*NA*		
Meghalaya	Ringkseh	Male	14	7	0	4	25	45
		Female	14	5	0	1	20	
	Kyton-u-Mon	Male	13	8	0	1	22	50
		Female	18	9	0	1	28	
	Total	Male	27	15	0	5	47	95
		Female	32	14	0	2	48	
Tripura	Beltali	Male	24	8	1	3	36	55
		Female	17	0	1	1	19	
	Kalitila	Male	19	10	0	7	36	54
		Female	13	3	1	1	18	
	Total	Male	43	18	1	10	72	109
		Female	30	3	2	2	37	
Grand Total		Male	70	33	1	15	119	204
		Female	62	17	2	4	85	

Table 7.44(a): Distribution of the Household Heads according to their Visit to Church/Temple

State	Village	Sex	Visiting Church/Temple			Sub Total	Total
			Everyday/At least once a week	Occasionally/ Rarely	Never/No Comments		
Meghalaya	Ringkseh	Male	14	9	2	25	45
		Female	11	6	3	20	
	Kyton-u-Mon	Male	17	3	2	22	50
		Female	20	5	3	28	
	Total	Male	31	12	4	47	95
		Female	31	11	6	48	
Tripura	Beltali	Male	4	25	7	36	55
		Female	3	9	7	19	
	Kalitila	Male	2	29	5	36	54
		Female	7	9	2	18	
	Total	Male	6	54	12	72	109
		Female	10	18	9	37	
Grand Total		Male	37	66	16	119	204
		Female	41	29	15	85	

Table 7.44(b): Distribution of the Counterparts of the Household Heads according to their Visit to Church/Temple

State	*Village*	*Sex*	*Visiting Church/ Temple*			*Sub Total*	*Total*
			Everyday/At least once a week	*Occasionally/Rarely*	*Never/No Comments*		
Meghalaya	Ringkseh	Male	10	2	4	16	35
		Female	11	7	1	19	
	Kyton-u-Mon	Male	2	3	15	20	41
		Female	1	4	16	21	
	Total	Male	12	5	19	36	76
		Female	12	11	17	40	
Tripura	Beltali	Male	3	8	6	17	53
		Female	13	18	5	36	
	Kalitila	Male	0	12	2	14	50
		Female	4	28	4	36	
	Total	Male	3	20	8	31	103
		Female	17	46	9	72	
Grand Total		Male	15	25	27	67	179
		Female	29	57	26	112	

number of the households in Meghalaya are Christian. We also get to know that only 4 male heads and 6 female heads in the surveyed villages never visited the church or temple. They were also not willing to state the reasons for this.

In Tripura at least 54 out of the total 72 male heads and 18 out of the 37 female household heads confirmed during the interview round with them that they visited the church/temple occasionally or rarely. Only 16 out of the total 109 household heads in the State frequented their place of worship regularly. Could it be that the villagers were influenced by the Marxist government in the State in matters of religion? (Fig. 7.73)

According to Table 7.44(b), while a maximum of the counterparts of the household heads in Ringkseh, Meghalaya went to their places of worship regularly, a maximum of them in Kyton-u-Mon either never went to the church/temple or were reluctant to reveal their stance or opinion.

In Tripura we find that unlike the female household heads in Beltali, the female counterparts in the same village felt more free to visit the temple/church regularly or occasionally, as was convenient for them. Again, quite a few of the female counterparts in Kalitila also frequented the places of worship occasionally.

8
Conclusion and Policy Implication

CONCLUSION

General Empowerment

In a country like ours, wherein parliamentary democracy is involved, it would be ideal if conditions could be created to the effect that women's voices are heard and their needs are recognized and prioritized, consequent to which their participation in diverse fields of activities is noticed by one and all. For such a situation, it is necessary that women should be empowered in various arenas such as social, political, economic, etc. Women need to be involved in the decision-making process also.

What Ought to be Done

- It is required to mount a determined campaign against the medical techniques to pre-birth sex-selection.
- A more detailed enumeration of the female-headed households is important for compiling reliable information on households headed by widows. It is essential to collect information on trends in widow remarriage. This could essentially focus on women's empowerment.
- Awareness generation programmes should be organized by the concerned government organizations as well as the non-government organizations in order to generate understanding among all sections of people, particularly

in the villages/districts to about the fact that the age of a girl during marriage should be at least 18 and that of a boy should be 21.

- Employment opportunities for women must be increased. A two-pronged effort is needed—first, to increase jobs for technically trained women; and second, to increase self-employment opportunities for technically trained women.

Economical Empowerment

In many families, even those women who comprise the salaried class, seldom have the freedom to decide how the money earned by self is to be spent. Most women do not have any control over the money earned by their husbands and other male family members. In many families, women, even though they are earning, have little or no say in economic decisions. So this lack of Economic Independence for women is to be addressed instantly.

What Ought to be Done

- Keeping in mind the displacement of female labour in agriculture, opportunities need to be created for off-farm agricultural employment.
- Surveys need to be conducted in order to know the reasons for the unemployment of the educated middle class women and measures need to be taken accordingly, on the basis of the findings.
- Training for new jobs and skill attainment need to be organized for women.

Political Empowerment

What Ought to be Done

- It is required to arrange awareness programmes on the equality in status between men and women, including in the basic rights as granted to them by the Constitution of India. Through these kinds of programmes, women would be conscious about their rights.
- The existing laws of the country on child marriages, sexual

harassment, physical torture, dowry, etc., should be amended, if necessary, in order to check the crimes being carried out.

Cultural and Social Empowerment

What Ought to be Done

- With direct or indirect initiatives by the State and Central governments, NGOs, Academic Institutions, Clubs and different organizations, festivals, exhibitions, seminars and discussions should be organized regularly to project on the need for prioritizing the cultural and social empowerment of women and to highlight the valuable contributions of women in different spheres of life.
- Literacy courses in the form of audiovisual programmes, through which the activities of women as well as their potential are highlighted in the media, should be organized in the local areas.
- Awareness about Panchayat, Social Organization, NGO, etc.. should be raised among women, especially in the rural areas. The women too are required to participate in these meetings/functions without fail.
- A woman's age of marriage having already been fixed at 18 years, her age of reproduction should also be fixed.
- Arrangements should be made to display the different local hand-made products that are prepared by women in different local fairs and festivals through which women could gain confidence and command respect while at the same time their products could be branded for marketization.

In spite of the fact that Meghalaya has a matrilineal society, we have observed that there are many male-headed households there; however, due to their involvement in academic and economic activities, the women in the State are more free and capacitated to participate in socio-cultural activities than their kinds in Tripura. Psychologically, they are highly placed and earn more respect. They do not need the permission of their male counterparts for taking part in outdoor activities. But then, the rural women suffer from discrimination against them in respect of nutritional intake.

In contrast, the women in Tripura are in a better off position comparatively, so far as their participation in political life is concerned.

Finally, we may state that there is immediate need to examine whether there is any correlation between education, income, job, etc., and the participation of women in social and cultural activities. Based on our findings, we can better understand the process of women's empowerment.

POLICY IMPLICATION

The Indian cultural norms that adversely affect female health and survival are the tendencies towards early marriage, early fertility, and preference for male children and lastly, but no less importantly, the neglect of the self, as traditionally practiced by women and girls. Social trends indicate that food, nutrition, and medical care always go in favour of the males. The high fertility rate among Indian women is risky for women's health, and anaemia, haemorrhage, toxaemia, sepsis and abortion are the major causes of maternal deaths. All the above facts have to be taken into consideration.

Poverty, malnutrition, illiteracy, population explosion and natural disasters are prominently discussed as the barriers for the development of any country and, accordingly, measures are taken to overcome these problems. However, many of these programmes are designed without giving necessary consideration to gender implications. To have a better country, an understanding of the multi-sectoral and interrelated impact on gender discrimination, which creates vulnerability of women at the national, regional and local levels, there is need for adopting short-term, medium-term and long-term strategies. Development initiatives should be based on the differential impacts of agricultural settings, forestry and deforestation, natural disasters and local governance on women, from the perspective of development.

For long, the need to increase women's capacity to participate in decision-making has been felt. It may be recommended here that there is an immediate need to strengthen the capacity of public institutions to integrate gender perspectives. In order to achieve the success of any programme, the introduction of participatory mechanisms is crucial. Given that women are producers towards subsistence and users of the forest and other common or environmental resources, there is a need to recognize and integrate women's knowledge and priorities in the conservation and management of such resources.

Some of the viable alternatives for achieving gender equality and development are suggested below:

- Recognize the gendered social construction;
- Recognize the social basis of power relations;
- Initiate researches through which accurate identification of women's biological, physical, socio-economic; and psychological vulnerabilities and capacities is possible; and
- Focus on both the problems and the capacities of women in different situations.

Some immediate requirements:

1. There is need for specific economic, social, agricultural and related policies in support of female household heads.
2. The skills of self-employed women should be upgraded through technology and financial assistance.
3. Land reforms should be implemented and joint land rights granted to women. Equal property rights for women in land should be ensured.
4. Leadership training should be arranged for all women and opportunities should be provided to them to encourage them to take leadership roles in civil society, both as students and adults.
5. Urgent actions should be taken to combat and eliminate violence against women resulting from harmful traditional practices, as it is in gross violation of their basic human rights.
6. The Government should ensure the public sector a primary role in providing basic services like health, education, transportation and sanitation.

Bibliography

Amartya Sen, *Development as Freedom*. Oxford University Press, New Delhi. 1999, p. 202.

________, 'Many Faces of Gender Inequality'. *Frontline*, 27th October-9th November, Chennai, 2001.

A.S. Altekar (1973), *The Position of Women in Hindu Civilization*. Motilal Banarasi Das, New Delhi.

Anupama Roy (2005), *Gendered Citizenship: Historical and Conceptual Exploration*. Orient Longman, New Delhi.

A.K. Adhikari (1978), Status and Role of Women among the Birthoer: A Nomadic Hunting and Gathering Community of Eastern India, in *Tribal Women in India*. Indian Anthropological Society, Calcutta.

Aditya Sen (1994), 'A Review of Women's Role in Panchayati Raj'. *Kurukshetra*, Vol. XLII, No. 9.

Asok Mitra, *Status of Women: Literacy and Employment*. ICSSR Programme on Women Studies, New Delhi, 1979.

________, *Status of Women: Household and Non-household Economic Activity*. CSSR Programme of Women's Studies, New Delhi, 1979.

Aparna Basu and Bharati Ray, *Women's Struggle: A History of the All India Women's Conference 1927-1990*. Manohar, New Delhi, 1990.

Atal Yagesh (1988), *Tribal Women and Development: An Epilogue In Tribal Women and Development* (ed.) by J.P. Sing *et al.*, Rawat Publication, Jaipur.

Bandopadhyaya and Mukherjee (1993), *New Horizon for West Bengal Panchayats.* A Report for Government of West Bengal, Department of Panchayats, Calcutta.

Banerjee, Nirmala, *Women Workers in the Unorganized Sector: The Calcutta Experience*. Sangam, Hyderabad, 1985.

_______ (ed.), *Indian Women in the Changing Industrial Scenario*. Sage Publications, New Delhi, 1991.

_______ *New Horizons for West Bengal Panchayats*. Government of West Bengal, Kolkata, 1993.

_______ and Devaki Jain (eds.), *Tyranny of the Household: Investigative Essays on Women's Work*. Shakti Books, Vikas Publishing House, New Delhi, 1985.

Bharati Ray and Aparna Basu, *From Independence towards Freedom: Indian Women since 1947*. Oxford University Press, New Delhi, 1999.

Bhaskar: Vol. II (1374 BE), Vol. III (1375 BE). Tripura Rabindra Parishad, Agartala.

Bina Agarwal, *A Field of One's Own: Gender and Land Rights in South Asia*. Cambridge University Press, New Delhi, 1994.

_______, Gender and Legal Rights in Landed Property in India. *Kali for Women*, New Delhi, 1999.

Boserup Esthar (1970), *Role of Women in Economic Development*. Allen & Unwin, London.

Bagchi Jasodhara (1999), "Women's Empowerment" In: *From Myth to Market*. edited by K. Sargari and U. Chakravarti. Manohar Publications, New Delhi.

Bhatt Anil (1977), "Dominant Caste and Political Process" in *Dimensions of Social Change*. (eds.), M.N. Srinivas *et al.* Allied Publishers, New Delhi.

Borale P.T. (1971), *Segregation and Desegregation in India*. Manaktalas, Bombay.

Bossard James H.S. (1944), "Marriage as Status Achieving Device" in *Sociology and Social Research*. 29 Sep.-Oct. New Delhi.

Choksi M. Armeane, *Foreword in Towards Gender Equality*. World Bank Publications. Washington D.C., U.S.A., 1995, p. 2.

D.N. (1989), 'Reservation of Seats for Women'. EPW, June 10.

Diwa Arora (1993), 'Power to the Women. *The Statesman*, April 7.

Das Veena (1976), *Indian Women: Work, Power and Status*. In Nanda (ed.)

Dumont Louis (1966), *Homo Hierarchicus*. Vikas Publication, Bangalore.

D'Souza V.S. (1974), Measurement of Rigidity-fluidity Dimension of Social Stratification in Six Indian Villages". *Sociological Bulletin*, Vol. XVIII. No. 1.

Emadi (1992), 'Women's Emancipation and Strategy Development in Albania'. *Economic and Political Weekly*, May 1.

G.K. Lieten, *Development, Devolution and Democracy: Village Discourse in West Bengal*. Sage Publication, New Delhi, 1996.

Government of India (1995), Fourth World Congress on Women, Beijing, 1995. *Country Report*, Department of Women and Child Development, Ministry of Human Resource Development, p. 116.

Gita Sen (eds.), Women's Empowerment and Demographic Process. *Moving Beyond Cairo*. Oxford University Press, New Delhi, 2000.

Gail Omvedt 1987, 'Women and Maharashtra Zilla Parishad Elections'. *EPW*, November 21.

Guha Sampa 1996, *Political Participation of Women in a Changing Society*. Inter-India, New Delhi.

Hall C.M. (1992), *Women and Empowerment: Strategies for Increasing Autonomy*. Hemisphere Pub. Corporation, Washington.

J.P. Singh (2000), 'Indian Democracy and Empowerment of Women'. *Indian Journal of Public Administration*, Oct-Dec.

Jain Devaki (1980), *Women's Quest for Power*. Five Indian Case Studies. Vikas Pub. New Delhi.

Jasodhara Bagchi ed. (1995), *Indian Women: Myth and Reality*. Sangam Books, Hyderabad.

Jeffrey Robin (1993), *Politics, Women and Wellbeing*. Oxford University Press, New Delhi.

K. Jayalakshmi (1996), *Empowerment of Women in Panchayats: Experiences of Andhra Pradesh*. NIRD, Hyderabad.

Kaushik Suheela (1991), 'Issues of Women's Development and Political Participation'. Teaching Politics, Vol. 17(1-2)

Kamla Nath and Milly Chatterjee, *Why Women? What Politics?*, Center for Social Research, New Delhi, 1996, p. 4.

Kanak Mukherjee, *Nari Andoloner Nana Katha Eksathe*. Kolkata, 1995.

_____ *Nari Mukti Andolan O Amra*. National Book Agency, Kolkata, 1999.

Leighley, Jan. 1991, 'Participation as Stimulus of Political Conceptualisation'. *Journal of Politics*, Vol. 53(1)

Leiten G.K. 1992(a), *Continuity and Change in Rural West Bengal*.

Sage Pub. New Delhi.

_______ 1992(b), 'Caste Gender and Class in Panchayats', *Economic and Political Weekly*, July 18.

_______ 1994(a), 'Rural Development in West Bengal London.

Mahbub. ul Haq (2000), *Human Development in South Asia: The Gender Question*. Human Development Center.

Neera Desai, *Women in Modern India*. Vora & Co., Bombay, 1957.

Conference on 'Gender Equality Through Women's Empowerment—Strategies and Approaches'. Lucknow, India, 1997.

Parthasarathi, V. (2002), *Inaugural Address on Women and Political Empowerment. Institute of Social Sciences*, New Delhi. p. 17.

Sahay K. (1998), *Women and Empowerment*. Discovery Publishing, New Delhi.

Sarkar Pabitra ed. (2001), *Bharater Samaj, Bharater Nari* (in Bengali). West Bengal State Book Board.

Sharma Kumud (1991-92), "Grass Roots Organisations and Women's Empowerment: Some Issues in the Contemporary Debate", in *Samya Shakti*. Centre for Women's Development Studies, New Delhi, Vol. VI, p. 29.

Simone De Beanvoir (1989), *The Second Sex*. Vintage Books, New York. South Asia Development Report, 2001.

Srinivas M.N. (1959), "The Dominant Caste in Rampura". *American Anthropologist*, Vol. 61, No. 1, New Delhi.

Srinivas M.N. (1962), *Caste in Modern India and Other Essays*. Asia Publishing House, New Delhi.

Srilatha Batliwala (1996), 'Empowering Women'. *Seminar, No. 449*, January.

Sen Choudhury S. (1995), *Women in Politics: West Bengal, A Case Study*. Minerva Pub, Calcutta.

Sujata Manohar, 'Gender Bias in Law Enforcement' in Workshop on Gender Bias in Law Enforcement. 10th Feb, 2001, p. 3.

Towards Equality: 1974 Report of the Committee on the Status of Women in India. Department of Social Welfare, Ministry of Education and Social Welfare, Government of India, December 1974.

Vina Majumdar (1989), 'Reservation of Seats for Women'. *EPW*, December 16.

_______ Enduring Conundrums: *India's Sex Ratio*, Essays in Honour of Asok Mitra. Rainbow Publications, New Delhi, 2001.

_______ *Symbols of Power: Studies on the Political Status of Women in India*. Allied Publishers, Bombay, 1979.

_______ V.B. Athreya and Ranjjeswari (no date), *Women's Participation in PR: A Case Study from Tamil Nadu*. M.S. Swaminathan Research Foundation, Chennai.

Vibhuti Patel (1994), 'Women and Structural Adjustment Programme in India'. *Social Scientist*, March-April.

Webster Neil (1992), *Panchayati Raj and the Decentralisation of Development Planning in West Bengal*. K.P. Bagchi, Calcutta.

_______ 1996, 'Panchayati Raj in West Bengal: Popular Participation for the People or the Party'. In Mathur (ed.), *Development Policy and Administration*. Sage Publications, New Delhi.

Appendix-I

Male and Female Household Heads at a Glance in Our Study Area in Tripura (Beltali+Kalitila) and Meghalaya (Kyton-u-Mon+Ringkseh)

Total	Meghalaya			Tripura		
	Male	Female	Total	Male	Female	Total
	47(49.47)	48(50.53)	95	72(66.06)	37(33.94)	109
Caste/Tribe/Religion						
General	0	0	0	19(70.4)	8(29.6)	27
SC	1(100)	0	1	24(55.8)	19(44.2)	43
OBC	0	0	0	12(75)	4(25)	16
Muslims	0	0	0	0	1(100)	1
Others/NA	3(50)	3(50)	6	17(77.3)	5(22.7)	22
Christian (ST)	41(51.25)	39(48.75)	80	0	0	0
Christian (Others)	2(25)	6(75)	8	0	0	0
Marital Status						
Unmarried	3(75)	1(25)	4	0	0	0
Married Once	36(67.9)	17(32.1)	53	71(79.8)	18(20.2)	89
Married more than once	4(80)	1(20)	5	1(100)	0	1
Widow	4(18.2)	18(81.8)	22	0	18(100)	18
Divorced	0	7(100)	7	0	0	0
Separated	0	4(100)	4	0	1(100)	1
Family Type						
Nuclear	4(57.1)	3(42.9)	7	0	5(100)	5
Joint	43(48.9)	45(51.1)	88	72(69.2)	32(30.8)	104
Earning Status						
Earner	3(25)	9(75)	12	8(32)	17(68)	25
Dependent	44(53)	39(47)	83	64(76.2)	20(23.8)	84
Age						
20-30	4(57.1)	3(42.9)	7	6(85.7)	1(14.3)	7

(Contd.)

Appendix I – *Contd.*

Total	Meghalaya			Tripura		
	Male	Female	Total	Male	Female	Total
31-40	12(57.1)	9(42.9)	21	24(92.3)	2(7.7)	26
41-50	8(47.1)	9(52.9)	17	17(70.8)	7(29.2)	24
51-60	10(50)	10(50)	20	14(58.3)	10(41.7)	24
61-70	11(50)	11(50)	22	7(38.9)	11(61.1)	18
> 70	2(25)	6(75)	8	4(40)	6(60)	10
Literacy Status						
Illiterate	7(28)	18(72)	25	10(31.2)	22(68.8)	32
< Madhyamik	26(53.1)	23(45.9)	49	50(76.9)	15(23.1)	65
> Madhyamik but <Graduate	11(68.8)	5(31.2)	16	11(100)	0	11
> Graduate	3(60)	2(40)	5	1(100)	0	1
Monthly Expenditure						
< 1499	2(25)	6(75)	8	2(33.3)	4(66.7)	6
1500-2500	6(31.6)	13(68.4)	19	19(61.3)	12(38.7)	31
2501-4000	14(60.9)	9(39.1)	23	34(75.5)	15(24.5)	49
4001-5000	9(50)	9(50)	18	7(70)	3(30)	10
> 5000	16(59.3)	11(40.7)	27	10(76.9)	3(23.1)	13
Family Size						
1-2	12(66.7)	6(33.3)	18	10(40)	15(60)	25
3-7	32(47.8)	35(52.2)	67	26(32.1)	55(67.9)	81
> 7	4(40)	6(60)	10	1(33.3)	2(66.7)	3

Appendix-II

Male and Female Household Heads at a Glance in Our Study Area in Tripura+Meghalaya (Grand Total)

Total	Meghalaya + Tripura		
	Male	Female	Total
	119(58.3)	85(41.7)	204
Caste/Tribe/Religion			
General	19(70.4)	8(29.6)	27
SC	25(56.8)	19(43.2)	44
OBC	12(75)	4(25)	16
Muslims	0	1(100)	1
Others/NA	20(71.4)	8(28.6)	28
Christian (ST)	41(51.2)	39(48.8)	80
Christian (Others)	2(25)	6(75)	8
Marital Status			
Unmarried	3(75)	1(25)	4
Married Once	107(75.4)	35(24.6)	142
Married more than once	5(83.3)	1(16.7)	6
Widow	4(10)	36(90)	40
Divorced	0	7(100)	7
Separated	0	5(100)	5
Family Type			
Nuclear	4(33.3)	8(66.7)	12
Joint	115(59.9)	77(40.1)	192
Earning Status			
Earner	11(29.7)	26(70.3)	37
Dependent	108(64.7)	59(35.3)	167
Age			
20-30	10(71.4)	4(28.6)	14
31-40	36(76.6)	11(23.4)	47

(Contd.)

Appendix II – *Contd.*

Total	Meghalaya + Tripura		
	Male	**Female**	**Total**
	119(58.3)	85(41.7)	204
41-50	25(61)	16(39)	41
51-60	24(54.5)	20(45.6)	44
61-70	18(45)	22(55)	40
> 70	6(33.3)	12(66.7)	18
Literacy Status			
Illiterate	17(29.8)	40(70.2)	57
< Madhyamik	76(66.7)	38(33.3)	114
> Madhyamik but <Graduate	22(81.5)	5(18.5)	27
> Graduate	4(66.7)	2(33.3)	6
Monthly Expenditure			
< 1499	4(28.6)	10(71.4)	14
1500-2500	25(50)	25(50)	50
2501-4000	48(66.7)	24(33.3)	72
4001-5000	16(57.1)	12(42.9)	28
> 5000	26(65)	14(35)	40
Family Size			
1-2	22(51.2)	21(48.8)	43
3-7	58(39.2)	90(60.8)	148
> 7	5(38.5)	8(61.5)	13

Appendix III

Distribution of Male and Female Household Heads in our Surveyed Area

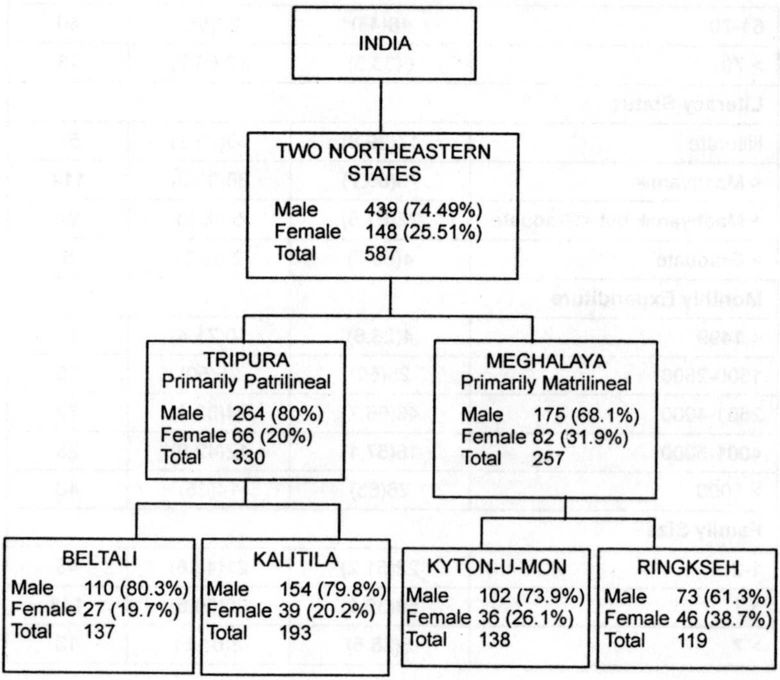

Index